Developing an Anti Harassment Corporate Policy: A Guide to Safe Workplaces

Surbhi Jain

SOCIETY Publishing

www.societypublishing.com

Developing an Anti Harassment Corporate Policy: A Guide to Safe Workplaces

Surbhi Jain

Society Publishing
224 Shoreacres Road
Burlington, ON L7L 2H2
Canada
www.societypublishing.com
Email: orders@arclereducation.com

ISBN: 978-1-77469-024-6 (Hardcover)

ABOUT THE AUTHOR

Dr Surbhi Jain is the Academic Director at TheWorldgrad She has a PhD (management) and an MBA (Marketing and HR). She has over 11 years of experience. She reads voraciously and writes eclectically. She has authored five books on Business communication, a prescribed textbook for the Mumbai university management course. This is in addition to 5 international research papers and three international case studies published within the last four years. She is a registered PhD Supervisor. She believes in encouraging young individuals to see the beauty and potential within them and encouraging deep love and respect for others and the environment.

TABLE OF CONTENTS

LIST OF FIGURES

LIST OF ABBREVIATIONS

ADA	Americans with Disability Act
ADEA	Age Discrimination in Employment Act
CEDAW	Convention on the Elimination of All Forms of Discrimination Against Women
CEO	Chief Executive Officer
CRST	Customer Requirement Support Team
CSIR	Council of Scientific and Industrial Research
EEOC	Equal Employment Opportunity Commission
EU	European Union
GINA	Genetic Information Non-discrimination Act
HR	Human Resource
HRTO	Human Rights Tribunal of Ontario
ICC	Internal Complaint Committee
IDHR	Illinois Department of Human Rights
IEC	Importer-Exporter Code
ILO	International Labor Organization
LCC	Local Complaints Committee
LGBTQ	Lesbian, Gay, Bisexual, and Transgender Queer
LLPs	Limited Liability Partnership
MNCs	Multinational Corporations
OCR	Office for Civil Rights
OEIG	Office of Executive Inspector General
OHRC	Ontario Human Rights Commission
POSH	Prevention of Sexual Harassment
RAND	Research and Development corporation
SAFE	Survey of Academic Field Experiences
SEQ	Sexual Experiences Questionnaire
SHRM	Society for Human Resource Management

U.S.	United States
UDHR	Universal Declaration of Human Rights
UN	United Nations
UNESCO	United Nations Educational, Scientific, and Cultural Organization

GLOSSARY

A

Ageism – discrimination or unfair treatment based on a person's age.
Aggrieved – feeling resentment at having been unfairly treated.
Agility ability to move quickly and easily.
Ample – generously sufficient to satisfy a requirement or need.
Apprentice – a person who is learning a trade from a skilled employer, having agreed to work for a fixed period at low wages.
Apprenticeships – the position of an apprentice.
Arbitrary – based on random choice or personal whim, rather than any reason or system.
Assuages – make (an unpleasant feeling) less intense.

B

Blue-Collar – relating to manual work or workers, particularly in industry.
Bystander – a person who is present at an event or incident but does not take part.

C

Coercion –is compelling a party to act in an involuntary manner by use of threats, including propaganda or force.
Colonialism – the policy or practice of acquiring full or partial political control over another country, occupying it with settlers, and exploiting it economically.
Conducive – making a certain situation or outcome likely or possible.
Contravention – an action which offends against a law, treaty, or other ruling.
Corporation – A big corporation or collection of corporations that is permitted to function as a single legal entity and is recognized as such by the government.
Counterparts – a person or thing that corresponds to or has the same function as another person or thing in a different place or situation.
Covenant – agree by lease, deed, or another legal contract.
Crippled – severely damaged or malfunctioning.
Cyberbullying – the use of electronic communication to bully a person, typically by sending messages of an intimidating or threatening nature.

D

Disciplinary – concerning or enforcing discipline.
Discourteous – showing rudeness and a lack of consideration for other people.
Discrimination – the unjust or prejudicial treatment of different categories of people, especially on the grounds of race, age, sex, or disability.

E

Endeavour – try hard to do or achieve something.

Epithets – an adjective or phrase expressing a quality or attribute regarded as characteristic of the person or thing mentioned.

F

Federal – having or relating to a system of government in which several states form a unity but remain independent in internal affairs.

Forbid – refuse to allow (something).

Forbidden – not allowed; banned.

Forum – a meeting or medium where ideas and views on a particular issue can be exchanged.

G

Gait – a person's manner of walking.

Genetic Information – the genetic potential of an organism carried in the base sequence of its DNA (or, in some viruses, RNA) according to the genetic code.

Globalization – The increasing interconnectedness of the world's economies, cultures, and inhabitants as a result of increased cross-border commerce in products and services, technology, and movements of investment, people, and information.

Graffiti – writing or drawings scribbled, scratched, or sprayed illicitly on a wall or other surface in a public place.

H

Harassment – if someone is abusing, insulting, or otherwise harming you on a regular basis, it is called harassment. Harassment is a word that describes any kind of ongoing torment. At school, harassment is often known as bullying. In the workplace, employees need to be careful about sexual harassment.

Homogenous – of the same kind.

Homophobia – dislike of or prejudice against gay people.

I

Infringe – actively break the terms of (a law, agreement, etc.).

Innuendos – an allusive or oblique remark or hint, typically a suggestive or disparaging one.

L

Lewdly – vulgar or sexually unchaste behavior.

M

Malicious – characterized by malice; intending or intended to do harm.

Mandated – give (someone) authority to act in a certain way.

Menace – a person or thing that is likely to cause harm; a threat or danger.

Menacing – suggesting the presence of danger; threatening.

Meticulous – showing great attention to detail; very careful and precise.
Misogyny – dislike of, contempt for, or ingrained prejudice against women.
Mitigating – having the effect of making something bad less severe, serious, or painful.
Mobbing – surrounding and attacking.
Mold – to make something into a particular shape or form by pressing it or by putting it into a mold.
Murky – obscure or morally questionable.

N
Nitty-Gritty – the most important aspects or practical details of a subject or situation.

P
Patriarchal – relating to or denoting a system of society or government controlled by men.
Patrol – an expedition to keep watch over an area, especially by guards or police walking or driving around at regular intervals.
Patrol Officers – people who work for the police service.
Perpetrators – a person who carries out a harmful, illegal, or immoral act.
Physiological – short-term changes in circulation, including blood pressure, heart rate, cardiac output, and vasoconstriction, as well as the release of stress hormones, including the catecholamines adrenaline and noradrenaline and cortisol, have been studied in experimental settings.
Policy – The course or principle of action adopted or proposed by an organization or individual.
Prosecution – the institution and conducting of legal proceedings against someone in respect of a criminal charge.
Psychological – psychology is the study of the mind and behavior, according to the American Psychological Association. It is the study of the mind, how it works, and how it affects behavior.
Pursuant – in accordance with (a law or a legal document or resolution).

Q
Quid Pro Quo – a favor or advantage granted in return for something.

R
Racism – the belief that different races possess distinct characteristics, abilities, or qualities, especially so as to distinguish them as inferior or superior to one another.
Ratified – sign or give formal consent to (a treaty, contract, or agreement), making it officially valid.
Reluctance – unwillingness or disinclination to do something.
Retaliation – the action of returning a military attack; counter-attack.

S
Scrutinizing – examine or inspect closely and thoroughly.

Seductive – seduction has multiple meanings. Platonically, it can mean "to persuade to disobedience or disloyalty," or "to lead astray, usually by persuasion or false promises." Strategies of seduction include conversation and sexual scripts, perilingual features, non-verbal communication, and short-term behavioral strategies.

Sensitizes – cause (someone or something) to respond to certain stimuli; make sensitive.

Sexism – prejudice, stereotyping, or discrimination, typically against women, on the basis of sex.

Solicitations – the act of asking for or trying to obtain something from someone.

Subsidiary – less important than but related or supplementary to something.

T

Taboo – a rule against doing or saying something in a particular culture or religion.

Transphobia – dislike of or prejudice against transsexual or transgender people.

Traumatic – deeply disturbing or distressing.

V

Vicarious – experienced in the imagination through the feelings or actions of another person.

PREFACE

This book takes the readers through several different concepts related to developing an anti-harassment corporate policy, an overview of harassment at the workplace, sexual harassment in academic sciences, engineering, and medicine. This book sheds light on the various organizational responsibility to prevent, prohibit, and redress sexual harassment at the workplace, on training, and policy creation and communication.

The first chapter stresses the anti-harassment corporate policy, workplace harassment, as well as their different types. This chapter will also emphasize the reporting of workplace harassment, preventing it, and implementing sexual harassment policies effectively.

The second chapter takes the readers through the basic overview of harassment at the workplace, its definition, identifying it and why it often occurs. This chapter will provide highlights on the consequences and remedies for workplace harassment, as well as its global overview.

Then, the third chapter explains the types of sexual harassment and describes it in light of academic sciences, engineering, and medicine, its reaction, and effects, how faculty and staff face it. This chapter also sheds light on the sexual harassment of trainees within sciences and medicine.

The fourth chapter introduces the readers to the organizational responsibility to prevent, prohibit, and redress sexual harassment at the workplace, developing a policy, duties of the employer under the prevention act. This chapter also explains the impact on complaints, instruments to check sexual harassment, and methods to stop it from occurring at the workplace.

The fifth chapter throws light on the several dimensions of anti-sexual harassment training, the requirement for the training, its significance. This chapter also contains different approaches to ensure that the training is effective and the troubles involved in it and provides information about retaliation.

The sixth chapter takes the readers through the concept of policy creation and communication, the policies and complaints of anti-harassment, a guide, and suggestions to write a code of conduct in the workplace. The readers are then told about the globalization and corporate anti-harassment policy and effectively and efficiently communicating such policies that are implemented and framed.

The last chapter of this book explains the issue of sexual harassment that takes place in a male-dominated workplace, along with addressing the acts and rules that are made for workplace harassment. This chapter also emphasizes the reasons why it flourishes, the factors that contribute to it. It also talks about the sexual harassment perpetrators, combating, and preventing it with different policies and training.

This book has been designed to suit the researcher and scholars' knowledge and pursuit and empower them with various aspects and concepts of anti-harassment and its corporate policies to update them with the information. I hope that the readers find the book explanatory and insightful and that scholars across various fields refer to this book.

Chapter 1

Introduction to Anti-Harassment Corporate Policy

CONTENTS

This chapter gives an insight to the reader about the anti-harassment corporate policy and an overview. It begins with stating the definitions of the workplace and harassment and defines them together in detail.

It discusses different types of workplace harassment, such as discriminatory harassment, based on religion, power, psychological, sexual, third-part, verbal as well as cyberbullying harassment.

The chapter highlights the measure for reporting workplace harassment, steps to prevent it. This chapter also states the definitions from the HR Anti-Harassment policy, and throws light on the racial and other types of harassment in the workplace.

As it proceeds further, it puts emphasis on the basic principles governing the anti-harassment policy along with describing the significance and benefits of prevention of sexual harassment (POSH) training.

It talks about the policy statement and anti-harassment as well as anti-discrimination policies, which includes descriptions and rationale, considerations, and elements.

1.1. INTRODUCTION

The ample work for everything depends on four pillars, in particular: giving social protection from the dangers in performing tasks and prioritizing the fundamental principles and rights at work (free from child labor, free from forced labor, non-discrimination, and freedom of association) without decreasing the opportunity to work along with giving the opportunity for social dialog.

The concept of non-discrimination as the essential right of laborers at work in industrial relations is focused on giving a favorable environment to work is specified in ILO Convention No. 100 concerning Equal Remuneration for Men and Women Workers for Work of Equal Value and ILO Convention no. 111 concerning Discrimination (Employment and Occupation) Convention, 1958 (No. 111).

In view of both ILO Conventions, laborers or workers reserve the privilege to get equivalent treatment without any exceptions, distinctions, or other choices dependent on national extraction, race, political beliefs, ethnicity, identity, ability, shading, sex, and color which resulted in the declining of equivalent opportunities in occupation, employment, or wages.

A comfortable working environment is very influential in accomplishing a favorable industrial relation. Something to be focused on in establishing a comfortable working environment is a working condition liberated from discrimination, which also includes liberation from sexual harassment at the workplace. As mentioned above, this is in line with the pillars in decent work.

At work, there has been no specific record of sexual harassment. Numerous elements influencing the accessibility of such records among others are: do not know where to register complaints, the feeling of fear, embarrassment, and various others.

With respect to this, the state has a function in encouraging the fulfillment of a comfortable working environment to all residents, particularly laborers, and to the individuals who are vulnerable to sexual harassment.

Sexual harassment at work is disadvantageous to all parties and could happen to anybody. For laborers, this could result in underperformance, which hence reduces work efficiency and affects the welfare of the laborers and their families. In this way, it is the prevailing concern to establish a comfortable working environment by preventing sexual harassment at work.

Thinking about such conditions, substantial measures are required to enhance the protection of women laborers from sexual harassment. From now on, the Government has evolved this Guideline on the prevention of sexual harassment (POSH) in the Workplace.

1.2. DEFINITIONS

To furthermore comprehend sexual harassment and its avoidance and requisite responses, the accompanying definitions pertain to sexual harassment at the workplace.

1.2.1. Harassment

Harassment is a type of employment discrimination that contravenes the Americans with Disabilities Act of 1990, (ADA), the Age Discrimination in Employment Act of 1967, (ADEA), and Title VII of the Civil Rights Act of 1964.

Harassment is unwanted behavior that depends on sex, race, religion, color, (counting pregnancy, gender identity, or sexual orientation), national origin, older age (starting at age 40), genetic information, or disability (including family medical history). Harassment becomes illegal where:

- Undergoing offensive behavior turns into a state of continued employment;

- The behavior is pervasive or severe enough to establish a workplace that a sensible individual would consider abusive, intimidating, or hostile.

Anti-discrimination laws additionally forbid harassment against people in reprisal for filing discrimination charges, testifying, or partaking in any way in a proceeding, investigation, or legal action under these laws, or contradicting employment practices that they sensibly accept as discriminate against people, in violation of these laws.

Trivial insults, isolated incidents, and annoyances (except if very serious) will not ascend to the level of illegality. To be illegal, the behavior should establish a work environment that would be offensive, hostile, or intimidating to reasonable individuals.

Offensive behavior may incorporate, yet is not restricted to, name-calling, slurs, offensive objects or pictures, offensive jokes, insults or put-downs, epithets, or physical assaults or threats, intimidation, and obstruction with the performance of work. Harassment can happen in a variety of conditions, including, yet not restricted to, the accompanying:

- The harasser can be the victim's co-worker, a non-employee, a supervisor in another area, an agent of the employer, or a supervisor;
- The victim can be anyone affected by the offensive conduct and does not have to be the person harassed;
- Illegal harassment may happen without economic injury to, or discharge of, the victim.

To eliminate harassment in the workplace, prevention is the best tool. Employers are urged to find proper ways to address and prevent unlawful harassment. They ought to evidently convey to workers that unwanted harassing behavior will not be allowed.

They can do this by building up a viable grievance or complaint process, giving anti-harassment training to their employees and managers, and taking appropriate and immediate actions when a complaint is filed by an employee.

Employers should endeavor to establish an environment in which workers will go ahead and raise concerns and are certain that those concerns will be tended to.

Employees are motivated to notify the harasser directly that the behavior must stop and is unwanted. Harassment should be reported to management at an early stage by an employee to prevent its escalation.

1.2.2. Workplace

In view of Law No. 1 of 1970, a place of work implies a physical place where each field or room, open or close, stationary, or movable, where laborers work or are regularly entered by labor for business and where there is a wellspring of risk, including all lawns, rooms, fields, and adjoining areas that comprises parts of, or are associated with the workplace (Figure 1.1).

Figure 1.1. An illustration of workplace.

Source: Image by Unsplash.com.

From the above definition, a place of work does not just incorporate physical places where work is performed during the eight working hours out of each day, for example, factories or offices.

A place of work additionally incorporates all areas where business-related business is directed because of an employment relationship or employment responsibilities, in areas, for example, work-related conference and training sessions, social functions, promotional campaigns, lunches, dinners organized for client or partners, and official business travel, communications through electronic media and telephone conversations.

Consequently, a place of work incorporates not just the physical room where work is performed for eight hours of the day, yet in addition all functioning hours outside of the eight working hours in the areas outside of an office-physical room.

1.3. WHAT IS WORKPLACE HARASSMENT?

Definition: Workplace harassment happens when a group of employees or an employee get belittled or feels threatened by their colleagues. The only motive of a workplace harasser is to make their victims feel uncomfortable and unsafe.

Workplace harassment goes by numerous names like-"workplace aggression," "mobbing," "workplace bullying," etc.

Harassment includes numerous types of segregation and demonstrations of contravention that is not constricted to one particular group. Harassment happens when people target numerous groups, including immigrants, women, people with disabilities, racial minorities, and sexual minorities. Basically, workplace harassment needs a pluralistic arrangement since it cannot be defined in one cognizant and solid definition.

1.4. TYPES OF WORKPLACE HARASSMENT

1.4.1. Discriminatory Harassment

This is a type of harassment that occurs based on protected clauses like sexuality, age, race, disability, gender, and religion. Further, it can be clarified as below:

- **Racial Harassment:** Because of their culture and race, an employee can be harassed. Straightforward slurs on their specific attributes of a certain ethnicity (nose shape, hair type, hair color, etc.). Showing disgust and disrespecting their culture is also a type of racial harassment.

For example, Connor who is Irish is called Carrot and Ginger because of his hair color.

- **Sexuality-based Harassment:** Because of their sexuality, an employee can be harassed. Workers who have sexual orientations like asexual, heterosexual, bisexual, homosexual, etc., may encounter this type of harassment.

For example, a homosexual woman may not be considered an efficient relationship therapist or a heterosexual man may face harassment working as a make-up artist (Figure 1.2).

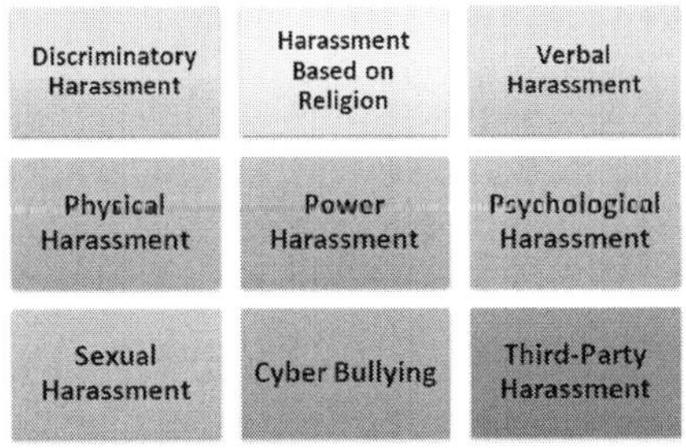

Figure 1.2. Types of workplace harassment.

- **Age-based Harassment:** An employee employed in an organization with a young trainee or apprentice or a younger workforce, and who is of mature age is not invited to social functions and meetings or who is made fun of, practical jokes, in the place of work can be considered as age-based discrimination.

For example, Bullying trainees.

- **Disability-based Harassment:** Discriminating or harassing an employee based on their mental or physical disability.

For example, teasing a person with down syndrome or imitating a crippled person's gait.

1.4.2. Harassment Based on Religion

Showing hatred, disrespect, and disgust to fellow employees because of their religious beliefs or religion.

For example, Managers not granting half-day or leave to Muslim workers on a religious holiday such as Eid al-Fitr.

1.4.3. Personal Harassment

This sort of harassment does not rely upon any protective clauses. Because of general disliking, a worker can be exposed to personal harassment by offensive jokes, intimidation tactics, inappropriate comments, personal humiliation, ostracizing behaviors, critical remarks, and so forth.

For example, the favoritism of staff who go out drinking with the boss makes Ralph feel that he is not appreciated and does not belong, who is a recovering alcoholic.

disturbing or humiliating messages, tagging in inappropriate memes, etc. This sort of harassment usually occurs after office hours, however can in any case be connected to the 'workplace.' Yes, having a tirade on Facebook on the grounds that the manager pulled an employee up for poor conduct during the day is not appropriate.

For example, even when the intern Sara clearly showed her disinterest, Shane messaging her repeatedly over a course of six months via the internet and social media to ask for a date.

Cyberbullying and digital harassment is the newest form of harassment. It is as derogatory as physical bullying, even though it happens online.

Sheri Mooney, CEO (Chief Executive Officer), and president of Mind Squad HR said:

"Digital harassment includes posting threats or demeaning comments on social media, creating a fake persona to bully someone online, creating a webpage about the victim to mock and belittle them, and making false allegations online."

In any workplace, usage of social media has become a norm. Hence, anyone can harass anyone digitally in the name of free speech. Individuals can make fake personas to bully or demean their colleagues.

However, there is also good news about digital harassment that victims can document it. Someone who encounters such discrimination and bullying can document these incidents in saved e-mails, screenshots, etc. By doing so, such offensive behaviors can be reported easily by the victims of workplace harassment.

1.5. HOW TO REPORT WORKPLACE HARASSMENT?

Each association has a HR department that is intended to assist workers who require assistance in serious situations. Good HR practices ensure employee's safety and job security, whenever they feel uncomfortable or in danger, or are threatened by a colleague.

Many harassing conducts or grievances lack physical proof, but that must not discourage a victim from filing an official complaint.

According to Mooney, it is necessary to report workplace harassment, as there may be complaints from other victims who might have reported similar offenses by the same offender. Most of the associations have strict anti-harassment policies and proper conduct policies, while on the other hand, few smaller associations may not. Organizations encourage employees, and most importantly, HR managers and leaders to take the below steps:

- With the harasser, try to have a one-to-one conversation calmly and ask him or her to stop directing such derogatory behavior towards the victims (employees). Although, if the abuse is physical, direct actions should be taken instead of approaching the harasser.
- If an employee file a complaint about harassment and it is seen that the harasser is in a leadership position, and the attempts to resolve it with the harasser fail, then the issue should be escalated to the attention of HR. Providing evidence should be considered if there are any, like text messages, eyewitnesses, or screenshots.
- If a manager feels that the company did not deal with the employees' complaints diligently, the EEOC should be contacted, which can evaluate the incident fairly. Employees should be assisted in getting in touch with them as they have their own agencies and laws regulating workplace conduct.

1.6. PREVENTING WORKPLACE HARASSMENT: FIVE PROACTIVE STEPS

Workplace harassment, in particular, sexual harassment in the work environment presently cannot seem to blur into the past. For instance, ongoing claims of worker sexual harassment surfaced at Uber, provoking an inquiry of a supposed hostile work environment to be driven by previous U.S. Head Attorney General Eric Holder.

> In two studies noted by The Daily Campus, one in every three women (in a survey of more than 2,000 women between the age group of 18 to 34) "reported encountering sexual harassment, and out of those, 71 percent of women refused to report it." As per a PwC survey of more than 25,000 women, 52 percent reported incidences of workplace harassment and bullying.

Visibly, the message has still to reach all U.S. businesses that it is illegal under Title VII of the Civil Rights Act to harass a person because of their gender and workplace harassment is bad for a company's culture and reputation. The definition of sexual harassment includes requests for sexual favors, unwelcome sexual advances, offensive remarks about a person's gender as well as various other physical or verbal harassment of a sexual nature. Businesses should also be aware of state laws forbidding harassment, which they may be obliged to comply with as well.

If the company has not come to terms with the potential for workplace harassment, this should become an immediate HR priority. The five proactive ways to help prevent harassment in the workplace that a business can implement, are discussed below: (Figure 1.3).

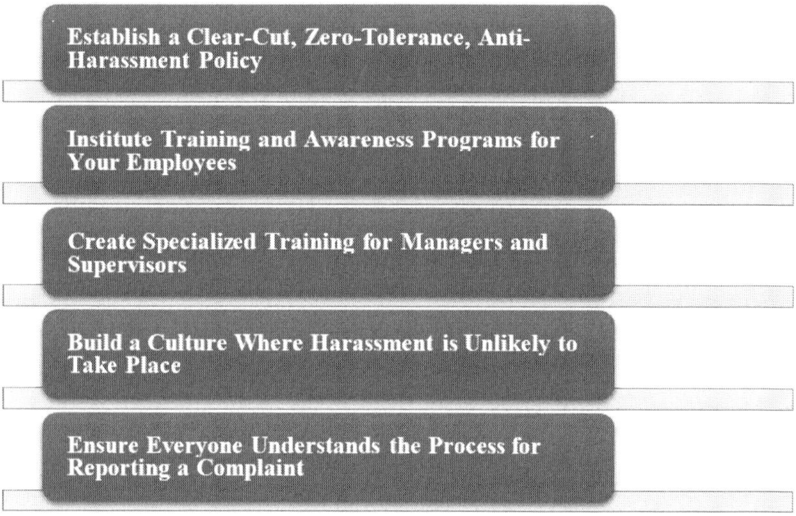

Figure 1.3. Proactive steps for preventing workplace harassment.

1.6.1. Establish a Clear-Cut, Zero-Tolerance, and Anti-Harassment Policy

An easy-to-understand and comprehensive anti-discrimination and anti-workplace harassment policy covering all employees should be crafted while working with the HR department. Organizations should make sure to include guidance from the company's legal counsel in order to guarantee the policy fully complies with federal, state, and local regulations and laws.

1.6.2. Institute Training and Awareness Programs for Your Employees

It is essential that each one of them throughout an association understands why an anti-workplace harassment policy is required and how a concerning situation can be reported by them. A training program should be scheduled on a regular basis, at least once or twice a year in which all employees must participate. This training should incorporate:

- What constitutes acceptable and unacceptable workplace behavior;
- How to recognize when sexual harassment takes place;
- Steps to take to report inappropriate behavior.

Melissa L said that "Just because a comment or action doesn't bother you doesn't mean it won't offend others around you." Wheeler, HRs consultant with Paychex HR Solutions stated that "It's not the intent that matters, it's the impact your actions have on the recipient."

1.6.3. Create Specialized Training for Managers and Supervisors

Evidently, people who are in charge of managing workers should behave immaculately in all workplace situations. Equally significant, they must be skilled in identifying when harassment happens and making clear under any circumstances, such behavior cannot be tolerated. This includes being sufficiently trained so that they are aware of (and know how to respond to) complaints of harassment, as well as understanding that either men or women can become a victim or instigate an illegal or highly inappropriate behavior. Such training is mandatory in some states.

1.6.4. Build a Culture Where Harassment Is Unlikely to Take Place

Business leaders should enforce and mold a culture where at all times, including offsite and off-hour gatherings, employees, and managers behave professionally. In such a culture, there is no place for demeaning or intimidating actions or offensive "humor" and those who are in charge presume the responsibility of continuously communicating their dedication to ensuring work in an environment free of harassment.

1.6.5. Ensure Everyone Understands the Process for Reporting a Complaint

In an employee handbook and at staff meetings, the process for filing a complaint of inappropriate behavior should be clearly laid out. Additionally, ensure everybody understands that each complaint is taken in a serious way and when necessary, an investigation will take place.

With the dedication of senior staff and leaders, it is feasible to set up a workplace environment in which harassing behavior and other unwelcome advances never happen or are handled swiftly, as need be. Eventually, all the employees will feel more secure and the business will be less likely to experience the harm to its reputation that comes in the form of a hostile work environment with claims of harassment.

1.7. DEFINITIONS FROM THE HR ANTI-HARASSMENT POLICY

1.7.1. Sexual Harassment

Sexual harassment is a form of sex discrimination. It is unlawful under federal and state law and is a violation of university policy. Under Title VII of the Civil Rights Act of 1964 and Title IX of the Education Amendments of 1972, sexual harassment is prohibited. Under Title VII to include sexual harassment, in the year 1980, the Equal Employment Opportunity Commission (EEOC) amended its "Guidelines on Discrimination Because of Sex."

It states that "requests for sexual favors, unwelcome sexual advances, and other physical or verbal conduct of a sexual nature amount to sexual harassment when:

- Acceptance of such behavior is made either implicitly or explicitly a condition or term of a person's employment;
- Rejection of such conduct or submission to such behavior by a person is utilized as the basis for employment decisions affecting such a person;
- Such behavior has the purpose or effect of substantially interfering with a person's work performance or creating an intimidating, offensive, or hostile working environment."

The Office for Civil Rights (OCR) of the Department of Education defines sexual harassment under Title IX and sets forth a policy stating that sexual harassment "consists of verbal or physical conduct of a sexual nature, imposed on the basis of sex, by an employee or agent of a recipient [of federal funds] that denies, limits, provides different, or conditions the provision of aid, benefits, services, or treatment protected under Title IX."

1.7.2. Racial and Other Harassment in the Work Environment

Under Title VII of the Civil Rights Act of 1964, harassment against people on the basis of their national origin, race, religion, or color is a form of unlawful discrimination and is prohibited. The EEOC "Guidelines on Discrimination Because of Sex," explicates that the principles for describing sexual harassment in the place of work apply as well to harassment based on a person's national origin, race, religion, or color.

When harassment based on a person's national origin, race, religion, or color has the "purpose or effect of substantially interfering with a person's work performance or establishing an offensive, hostile, intimidating working environment," it rises to the level of illegal discrimination.

Additionally, these principles apply to harassment on the basis of genetic information, age, and disability under the Genetic Information Nondiscrimination Act, the ADEA, and the Americans with Disabilities Act, respectively.

Ultimately, the University, through its nondiscrimination statement, implements these principles to prevent harassment on the basis of an individual's gender expression, sexual orientation, and gender identity.

In compliance with federal law, Vanderbilt University does not retaliate against people for:

- Filing or encouraging an individual to file a complaint of illegal discrimination;
- Engaging in an investigation of illegal discrimination;
- Opposing illegal discrimination.

In addition, the University does not retaliate against people for filing or encouraging one to participate in an investigation of discrimination, file a complaint of discrimination, or opposing discrimination based on grounds not necessarily protected by state or federal law, but protected by the University's non-discrimination policy, such as sexual orientation.

"Retaliation" includes any adverse employment action or act of revenge against a person for filing or encouraging one to file a complaint of discrimination, participating in an investigation of discrimination, or opposing discrimination:

- The Genetic Information Non-discrimination Act of 2008 (GINA) forbids discrimination in employment and in health coverage based on genetic information.

- Sexual orientation refers to an individual's self-identification as pansexual, bisexual, heterosexual, asexual, homosexual, or uncertain.
- Gender identity is usually defined as an individual's own sense of identification as female, male, both, or neither as distinguished from actual biological sex, i.e., it is one's psychological sense of self.
- Gender expression is everything everyone does that communicates their sense of identification to others.

1.8. BASIC PRINCIPLES GOVERNING THE ANTI-HARASSMENT POLICY

The basic principles that govern the anti-harassment policy are the following:

- In compliance with the standards of conduct for the International Civil Service, all the employees of UNESCO (United Nations Educational, Scientific, and Cultural Organization.) shall treat each other fairly, with courtesy, dignity, and respect, without physical or verbal abuse, regardless of contractual status or rank.
- At UNESCO, harassment shall not be tolerated, which is committed to establishing an environment free of harassment or abuse of authority. Every employee will contribute to such an environment.
- The focus shall be put on preventive action against harassment. The early detection of harassment and swift action to stop it should also be prioritized. Prevention of harassment is a shared individual and organizational responsibility.

Every UNESCO representative, at any level, and specifically at the supervisory level, is accountable for building a positive workplace and an environment of tolerance and trust, free from all types of harassment. An organization is also responsible for the prevention and resolution of harassment and it should also ensure that appropriate mechanisms are in place.

- All complaints of harassment are treated seriously. To this effect, even if there are no formal complaints, management is committed to resolving all instances of harassment as soon as it becomes aware of them. Before an incident becomes pervasive or severe, employees should, therefore, report all incidents of harassment in the workplace.

- If it is proven, harassment should be sanctioned and disciplinary measures should be taken against the harasser. If a manager knowingly tolerates harassment once he or she has become aware of it, sanctions may also be imposed against him or her.

On the other hand, employees must keep in mind that all allegations of harassment are very serious, and deliberately malicious or false allegations shall be sanctioned. Therefore, before making a complaint of harassment, they must therefore have serious grounds. Such complaints must be based on facts. The alleged harasser has the duty and right to respond to allegations of harassment.

1.9. HOW TO EFFECTIVELY IMPLEMENT A SEXUAL HARASSMENT POLICY?

Implementation of an efficient sexual harassment policy is the best way to evade EEOC claims and lawsuits down the road; this topic of the chapter is about how to do it.

When a formal charge of sexual harassment is filed with the EEOC or the Hawaii Civil Rights Commission, or a sexual harassment lawsuit is brought in federal court or Hawaii State court, one primary issue will be what (if anything) the employer did to prevent or stop the harassment.

There are various steps for an employer that he or she should take to emphasize to employees that sexual harassment will not be tolerated in the offices or workplace. The management executives or supervisors of an employer play a very significant role in executing each of these steps.

Out of many, one of the most important things an employer can do is to implement an efficient sexual harassment policy, which is consisting of a procedure for employees that helps to file complaints against the harassment (Figure 1.4).

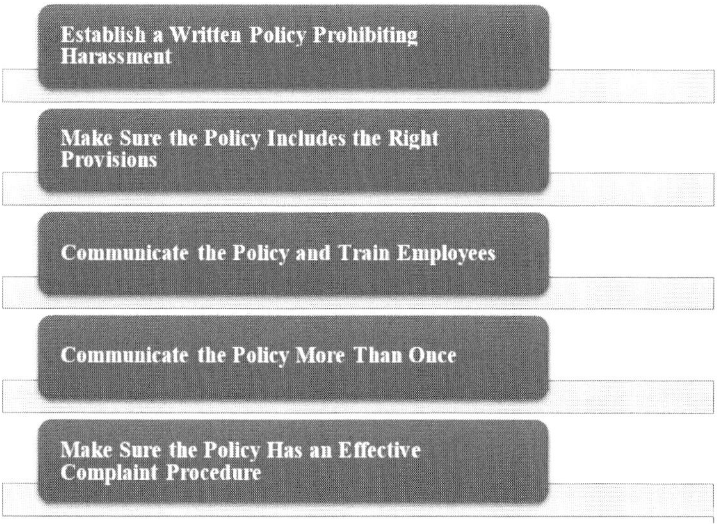

Figure 1.4. How to effectively implement a sexual harassment policy?

1.9.1. Establish a Written Policy Prohibiting Harassment

It should be the duty of every employer to make sure that they have a written policy specifically about prohibiting sexual harassment. The policy should be highlighted or included in the employee handbook, and must be distributed to all new employees, posted, redistributed on a regular basis, and communicated to employees frequently.

1.9.2. Make Sure the Policy Includes the Right Provisions

The policy should include language which:

- States that sexual harassment will not be tolerated;
- Explains and gives examples of sexual harassment and other prohibited conduct;
- Highlights a procedure for employees in order to file complaints about the sexual harassment, and motivates all employees (not just victims of harassment) to report incidents of unwelcome sexual conduct;
- Provides various avenues for an employee to file a complaint against sexual harassment, in such a way that the employee can bypass his or her supervisor, who might be the alleged harasser;

- Makes sure that all complaints will be handled as confidentially as possible;
- Ensures that employees who is filing the complaint about sexual harassment will not suffer adverse job consequences (retaliation) as a result of the complaint;
- States that any employee who engages in unwelcome sexual conduct is subject to discipline, up to and including discharge; and
- Requires supervisors and managers to immediately report suspected sexual conduct.

Management executives and supervisors must become entirely familiar with the policy prohibiting sexual harassment provided by the employer. They should re-read the policy on a regular basis and consult the policy when any sexual harassment issue arises.

1.9.3. Communicate the Policy and Train Employees

Moreover, when providing the policy to each and every employee, the policy should be read and described to employees in group meetings. Employees should be educated in order to distinguish and confront harassment.

Management executives and supervisors should be trained to impose the policy, sensitized to recognize improper conduct among associates and colleagues when it occurs, and educated about taking the suitable actions in order to stop and remedy the misconduct.

1.9.4. Communicate the Policy More Than Once

In order to be an efficient tool against the sexual harassment, the policy must be clearly communicated to employees on a regular basis. This can be done formally with the help of employee group meetings and informally with the help of managers' and supervisors' conversations with their reports.

Management executives and supervisors can also take an active participation in the communication process by necessitating the employees to attend the training, following up with employees on what they have learned or gained knowledge at the training session, asking questions regarding the training and the policy, and providing positive responses to employees who have participated in the employer's efforts in order to stop and eliminate the sexual harassment in the workplace.

After a policy against the sexual harassment has been announced, management executives and supervisors must also take the follow-up action in order to ensure that employees are not engaging in prohibited activity. If a meeting is held telling employees to stop certain behavior, it is the duty of management executives and supervisors to make sure that the meeting has been taken seriously by the employees or people who have attended the session.

1.9.5. Make Sure the Policy Has An Effective Complaint Procedure

A complaint procedure or policy should motivate employees to come forward with the allegations of sexual harassment. There should be numbers of people to whom an employee can bring an initial complaint.

HRs officers or the other suitable employer representatives should be appointed to investigate the complaints. There should also be a minimum of two potential investigators, in the event one is the accused harasser. In addition to this, it is a good idea to appoint both men as well as women, as the investigators, because the complainant might feel more comfortable or they could be more specific while reporting the conduct to someone of the same sex.

Management executives and supervisors must take any complaint of sexual harassment that they receive seriously. They should instantly report the complaint to the HRs or any other company representative who is in charge of the EEOC-compliance responsibilities.

And then, they should guarantee employees that no retaliation will be taken against anyone who has filed the complaint and that their complaints will be handled as discreetly as it could be possible. They should also tell anyone who complains that their allegations will be promptly and thoroughly investigated.

1.10. IMPORTANCE AND BENEFITS OF PREVENTION OF SEXUAL HARASSMENT TRAINING (POSH) FOR THE EMPLOYEES

Regardless of whether they are large corporations or small companies, modern businesses must guarantee adequate HR services to avoid sexual harassment in the workplace. One of the unwanted issues in the business setting is sexual harassment in the place of work leading to dangerous and serious consequences. One of the crucial requirements of HR Compliance is mandatory sexual harassment prevention training.

1.10.1. The Significance of Sexual Harassment Prevention Training

Today, one of the major concerns of business owners is work-related sexual harassment. Not only the corporate environment, even family-held companies, and small-sized businesses are faced with such issues. Sexual harassment prevention training for employees has become inevitable. Together with adopting stringent policies, effective training sessions given by professional HR training and consultancy are now an essential element in business (Figure 1.5).

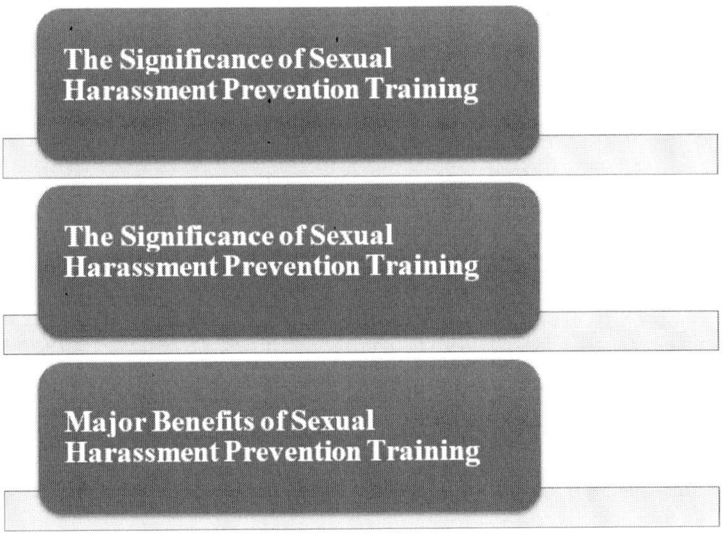

Figure 1.5. Importance and benefits of prevention of sexual harassment training (POSH) for your employees.

To fight the rising workplace harassment accusations and complaints, regular, and strong training needs to be given by experienced and skilled HR services. Such training serves numerous purposes, such as mitigating risk related to legal liability, educating the employees, and meeting legal compliance at the workplace.

1.10.2. The Significance of Sexual Harassment Prevention Training

- ***Employees are Protected*:** Having a zero-tolerance policy and giving appropriate training empowers the employees and makes them feel comfortable at work.
- ***Training Helps Improve Morale*:** Taboo, as it might sound, the issue of sexual harassment must be addressed head-on and should not be considered Taboo. Sexual harassment prevention training through strong HR services ensures that employees of an organization feel more confident and committed.
- ***Companies are Protected from Legal Liability*:** Sexual harassment at the workplace is greatly reduced because of regular training. This has resulted in reduced legal liability for the business organization.
- ***Employee Productivity Increases*:** Providing effective training with professional HR training and consultancy makes employees feel more valued. This translates into a more committed workforce which, in turn, increases the productivity of employees.
- ***The Expected Behavior is Achieved*:** Training imparts culture and discipline. Standardized training conducted by expert HR services will ensure HR compliance and develops and defines acceptable behavior among employees.

1.10.3. Major Benefits of Sexual Harassment Prevention Training

- ***The Work Environment Becomes Safer*:** Sexual harassment causes stress and it is instrumental in creating an unsafe workplace. Training can eliminate the feelings of fear and discomfort created by this. This guarantees a safe work environment that assures profits, quality, and efficiency.
- ***Workplace Culture is Strengthened:*** By communicating the values, goals, and policies of an organization to its various members, training strengthens organizational culture and motivates people.
- ***Training Encourages Reporting and Empowers Bystanders*:** When effective training is provided, the otherwise unreported harassment and discrimination will come out to the open. Not

just the employees, the bystanders are also educated about the accepted and expected conduct in the workplace.

- ***Compliance Risk is Reduced*:** The business is at a potential legal, financial, and professional risk that might prove expensive when the workforce is ignorant and untrained of sexual harassment issues. Training saves the business from the outcomes of such factors.

1.11. POLICY STATEMENT

An important element in the successful execution of the POSH in the place of work is a strong commitment from all the levels in the organization or enterprise, starting from level executives, supervisors, managers, until the executor.

In order to create a positive working environment that is conducive to the enterprise or organization, a policy statement on sexual harassment is a message from management to employees which states the philosophy, policies, and the company's commitment to manage and prevent sexual harassment.

The policy statement should come from upper management to make sure the policy is observed and accepted by the managers, employees, and supervisors throughout the workplace. The policy statement should contain all the following points:

- The declaration that all job applicants, workers, and any third party connected with the company reserve the right to be treated with dignity and without any distinction.
- A full explanation of all forms of behaviors that constitute sexual harassment.
- An assertion that sexual harassment is not condoned or permitted in the organization on the principle of zero tolerance.
- An assurance that all people who have been subjected to sexual harassment at the place of work have a right to raise their complaints and adequate action shall be taken in accordance with the stipulation in the company.
- A detailed explanation of the procedure which should be followed by employees who are victims of sexual harassment, and the management and employees who are tasked to manage complaints.

- An affirmation stating that sexual harassment constitutes a breach of the enterprise's policy and will incur disciplinary actions in accordance with the agreement in the company.
- A directive stating that managers and supervisors have a positive responsibility to execute the policy and to demonstrate leadership by example.

1.12. ANTI-HARASSMENT AND ANTI-DISCRIMINATION POLICIES

1.12.1. Description and Rationale

Anti-discrimination and anti-harassment policies make it very clear that discrimination and harassment will not be allowed and supported, and set expectations and standards for behavior. An anti-discrimination or anti-harassment policy should explain the types of behavior that are harassing or discriminatory, and pass on the message that these concerns are taken very seriously.

The policy should also elucidate the responsibilities and roles. These human rights policies ought to be linked to already existing policies of an organization and integrated into the way the association operates on a daily basis.

1.12.2. Considerations

Harassment is considered a specific form of discrimination. Various organizations have separate policies for harassment and for other forms of discrimination because harassment raises unique issues.

As well, since discrimination and harassment related to the numerous Code grounds often manifest themselves differently, few associations have particular policies related to harassment and/or discrimination on the basis of gender expression, sexual orientation, gender identity, race, and race-related grounds, and sex, etc. (Figure 1.6).

Anti-discrimination and anti-harassment policies set out standards and expectations, and on the other hand, complaint procedures set out if there is a potential violation of these policies then how will it be addressed. Numerous organizations choose to combine their anti-discrimination and anti-harassment procedures and policies into a single document.

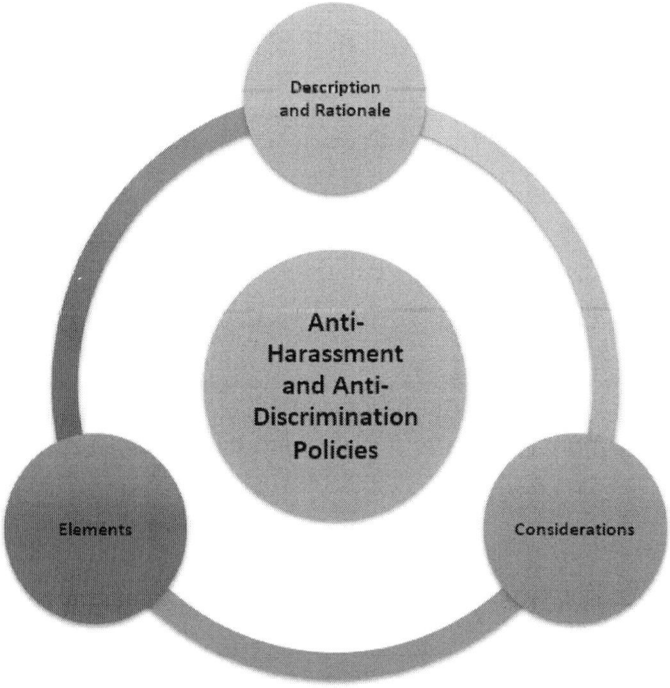

Figure 1.6. Anti-harassment and anti-discrimination policies.

Additionally, associations can develop a policy on competing rights to address situations where rights in the place of work may come into conflict. This policy can be part of broader anti-harassment and anti-discrimination policies or a separate document. The OHRC's (Ontario Human Rights Commission) policy on competing rights gives guidance as to what this type of organizational policy should contain.

1.12.3. Elements

1.12.3.1. Organization Commitment

A policy should contain a clear statement of the organization's commitment to create and maintain respect for human rights, and fostering equality and inclusion.

XYZ Organization is committed to giving an environment free of harassment and discrimination and, where all people are treated with dignity and respect, can have equal opportunities, and contribute fully.

Every person has the right to be free from discrimination and harassment under the Ontario Human Rights Code. At XYZ Organization, discrimination, and harassment will not be ignored, tolerated, or condoned. If a claim of discrimination or harassment is proven, disciplinary measures will be taken, which may even include termination of employment.

XYZ Organization is committed to a comprehensive strategy to address discrimination and harassment, including:

- Providing education and training to ensure everyone knows their responsibilities and rights;
- Regularly monitoring organizational systems for barriers relating to Code grounds;
- Providing a fair and effective procedure for complaints;
- At all times, promoting appropriate standards of conduct.

1.12.3.2. Policy Objectives

The policy should set out its objectives, such as defining principles and standards for behavior, preventing discrimination and harassment, and promoting human rights within the organization.

The objectives of this policy are to:

- Ensure that associates, members, and clients of XYZ Organization know that discrimination and harassment are intolerable practices and are incompatible with the standards of the organization, as well as being it is a violation of the law;
- Set out the types of conduct that are prohibited and may be considered offensive by this policy.

1.12.3.3. Applying the Policy

The policy should set out the activities involved and who it applies to. For example, in employment, Code protections have been interpreted broadly, to include contract, casual, temporary staff, and volunteers. Employees are protected against discrimination and harassment by co-workers, superiors, and management, and they are also protected from the actions of others like suppliers or clients, who enter the employment context.

Employees may be protected outside of normal working hours or while off the worksite, where activities are connected to the place of work. Because employees are entitled to work in an environment free of discrimination and harassment from suppliers, clients, or others who enter the employment context, make it available to visitors or publicly post the policy.

The Code also wants organizations to prevent discrimination and harassment in the services they offer to the public. This includes dealings with potential customers, business associates, customers, and suppliers.

The right to be free from harassment applies both to applicants and tenants, in rental housing. Landlords may be held liable if they do not take necessary steps to make sure that tenants are protected from harassment by people visiting the premises, for example, maintenance, and other support staff and by other tenants.

The right to freedom from harassment and discrimination extends to all the employees, including contract, full-time, probationary, part-time, casual, and temporary staff, as well as apprentices, volunteers, interns, and co-op students.

Additionally, it is unacceptable for employees of XYZ Organization to engage in discrimination or harassment when dealing with clients, or with others, they have professional dealings with, such as service providers or suppliers.

This policy applies to every aspect of the employment relationship and the workplace environment and at every level of the organization, including salaries, training, recruitment, transfers, promotion, selection, benefits, and termination. It also covers performance evaluations, rates of pay, discipline, overtime, shift work, hours of work, and holidays.

This policy also applies to events that happen outside of the physical place of work such as during company parties or business trips.

1.12.3.4. List and Explain Protected Grounds

The human rights code prohibits discrimination in five parts of society, called "social areas"-vocational and professional associations, employment, contracts, and membership in trade, housing, services. Protection is offered based on 17 grounds.

Applicable Code grounds along with definitions should be set out where necessary. Depending on the social area involved it should be noted that the Code grounds vary somewhat. The ground of "receipt of public assistance" applies only in housing while the ground of "record of offenses" applies only in the social area of employment.

While the Code prohibits discrimination because of pregnancy under the ground of sex, as many are unaware of this Code protection, it may be helpful for policies to explicitly identify harassment and discrimination based on pregnancy.

The policy can also note that people may encounter harassment and discrimination on the basis of the intersection of multiple grounds of discrimination (intersectionality). Such as, an individual who encounters harassment on the grounds that she is a Muslim woman can file a complaint based on both creed and sex.

Apart from that mandated by the Code, organizations may choose to extend protection further. For example, some organizations prohibit any form of harassment based on political opinion and psychological discrimination and harassment.

This policy prohibits harassment or discrimination based on the following grounds and any combination of these grounds:

- Sexual orientation;
- Age;
- Creed (religion);
- Sex (including pregnancy and breastfeeding);
- Family status (such as being in a parent-child relationship);
- Race;
- Gender identity;
- Gender expression;
- Marital status (including married, single, widowed, divorced, separated, or living in a conjugal relationship outside of marriage, whether in a same-sex or opposite-sex relationship);
- Disability (including mental, physical, developmental, or learning disabilities);
- Color;
- Ancestry;
- Place of origin;
- Ethnic origin;
- Citizenship;
- Record of offenses (criminal conviction for a provincial offense, or for an offense for which a pardon has been received);

- Relationship or association with a person identified by one of the above grounds;
- The perception that one of the above grounds applies.

1.12.3.5. Define Key Concepts

Consistent with human rights law and policy. Offer examples to clarify the concepts. It could be helpful to give definitions of related concepts, for example, ageism, racism, heterosexism, etc., and to outline common manifestations of discrimination related to specific Code grounds. for more information, consult the relevant OHRC policies.

It is significant to note that people encountering harassment may not object outwardly to the harassing conduct or comments. People may feel unable to object. For example, they may be afraid of the consequences of speaking out or be in a vulnerable situation. It does not matter if anyone voices objections, not to the person making the offensive comments, they can still make a complaint and the behavior can still be found to be harassment.

The following behavior is prohibited:

- *Discrimination*: It means based on a Code ground, any type of unequal treatment, whether denying benefits or imposing extra burdens. It may be unintentional or intentional. It may involve procedures, rules, or practices that appear neutral but are disadvantageous for certain groups of people or direct actions that are discriminatory on their face.

Discrimination may happen in very subtle ways or it may take obvious forms. Even if there are many components affecting an action or decision, if discrimination is one component, then it is a violation of this policy.

- *Harassment*: This means a course of actions or comments that are known or ought reasonably to be known, to be unwelcome. It can involve actions or words that are known to be unwelcome, offensive, demeaning, embarrassing, or humiliating, based on a ground of discrimination recognized by this policy. Based on any of the grounds of discrimination, harassment can happen.

Examples of harassment include:

- Epithets, innuendos, remarks, or jokes related to an individual's age, race, creed, gender identity, sexual orientation, gender expression, disability, sex, or any other ground;

- Circulating or posting or offensive materials, pictures, or graffiti, whether via e-mail or in print form or other electronic means;
- Singling out a person for degrading or humiliating jokes or teasing because they are a member of a Code-protected group;
- Comments ridiculing an individual because of characteristics that are related to a ground of discrimination. For example, this could involve comments about a person's speech, dress, or other practices that may be related to their creed, sex, gender identity, or race.

The behavior is not considered okay if a person does not explicitly object to harassing behavior, or appears to be going along with it. Under the Code, the behavior could still be considered harassment.

- *Sexual and Gender-based Harassment*: sexual harassment is a form of harassment that can include:
- Gender-related comments about a person's mannerisms or physical characteristics;
- Paternalism based on gender which an individual feels undermines his or her position of responsibility or self-respect;
- Unwelcome physical contact;
- Offensive or suggestive innuendos or remarks about members of a particular gender;
- Propositions of physical intimacy;
- Gender-related taunting, verbal abuse, or threats;
- Leering or inappropriate staring;
- Bragging about sexual prowess or discussions or questions about sexual activities;
- Offensive comments or jokes of a sexual nature about a client or an employee;
- Rough and vulgar humor or language related to gender;
- Display of sexually offensive graffiti, pictures, or other materials including through electronic means;
- Demands for dates or sexual favors.
- *Sexual Solicitation*: This policy prohibits sexual solicitations or advances by any individual who is in a position to deny or grant a benefit to the recipient of the solicitation or advance. This includes supervisors and managers, as well as colleagues where

18. Ministry of Manpower and Transmigration, (2011). Guidelines on Sexual Harassment Prevention at the Workplace. [eBook] Indonesia: Ministry of Manpower and Transmigration. Available at: https://www.ilo.org/wcmsp5/groups/public/---asia/---ro-bangkok/---ilo-jakarta/documents/publication/wcms_171329.pdf (accessed on 17 August 2021).

19. Nielsen, M., Madsen, I., Clausen, T., Skov, S., Kjær, S., Kvorning, L., Aldrich, P., Rugulies, R., & Folker, A., (2019). Sexual harassment at work: Design of a new questionnaire to measure sexual harassment. European Journal of Public Health, [Online] 29(4). Available at: https://academic.oup.com/eurpub/article/29/Supplement_4/ckz186.327/5623691 (accessed on 17 August 2021).

20. Ontario Human Rights Commission, (n.d.). 5. Anti-Harassment and Anti-Discrimination Policies | Ontario Human Rights Commission. [Online] Ohrc.on.ca. Available at: http://www.ohrc.on.ca/en/policy-primer-guide-developing-human-rights-policies-and-procedures/5-anti-harassment-and-anti-discrimination-policies (accessed on 17 August 2021).

21. Paychex, (2017). Preventing Workplace Harassment: 5 Proactive Steps. [Online] Paychex. Available at: https://www.paychex.com/articles/human-resources/workplace-harassment-prevention (accessed on 17 August 2021).

22. Sahai, S., Goel, R., & Punni, M., (2020). Behavioral and emotional dimensions of sexual harassment at workplace. Emotion and Information Processing, [Online] pp. 79–95. Available at: https://link.springer.com/chapter/10.1007%2F978-3-030-48849-9_6 (accessed on 17 August 2021).

23. Sentrient Blog, (2021). 10 Types of Workplace Harassment That Can Put Your Business at Risk | Sentrient Blog. [Online] Sentrient Blog. Available at: https://www.sentrient.com.au/blog/11-types-workplace-harassment-can-put-business-risk (accessed on 17 August 2021).

24. Shaikh, D., (2019). Sexual harassment and the laws relating to the sexual harassment. SSRN Electronic Journal, [Online] Available at: https://papers.ssrn.com/sol3/papers.cfm?abstract_id=3394422 (accessed on 17 August 2021).

25. Talentpro India, (2021). Importance and Benefits of Prevention of Sexual Harassment Training (POSH) for Your Employees | Talentpro India. [Online] Talentpro India. Available at: https://www.talentproindia.

com/2021/04/27/importance-and-benefits-of-prevention-of-sexual-harassment-training-for-your-employees-posh/ (accessed on 17 August 2021).

26. Tang, T., & McCollum, S., (1996). Sexual harassment in the workplace. Public Personnel Management, [Online] 25(1), 53–58. Available at: https://journals.sagepub.com/doi/10.1177/009102609602500105 (accessed on 17 August 2021).
27. Tinsley, H., & Stockdale, M., (1993). Sexual harassment in the workplace. Journal of Vocational Behavior, [Online] 42(1), 1–4. Available at: https://www.sciencedirect.com/science/article/abs/pii/S0001879183710018?via%3Dihub (accessed on 17 August 2021).
28. U.S. Equal Employment Opportunity Commission, (2021). Harassment | U.S. Equal Employment Opportunity Commission. [Online] Eeoc.gov. Available at: https://www.eeoc.gov/harassment (accessed on 17 August 2021).
29. UN.org. (n.d.). 16.2. Anti-Harassment Policy. [Online] Available at: https://www.un.org/womenwatch/osagi/UN_system_policies/(UNESCO)Anti-harassment_Policy.pdf (accessed on 17 August 2021).
30. Vanderbilt University, (2021). Definitions from the HR Anti-Harassment Policy. [Online] Vanderbilt University. Available at: https://www.vanderbilt.edu/genderharassment/definitions/definitions-from-the-hr-anti-harassment-policy/ (accessed on 17 August 2021).
31. Yorker, B., (1992). Sexual harassment in the workplace. AAOHN Journal, [Online] 40(11), 550–554. Available at: https://journals.sagepub.com/doi/10.1177/216507999204001107 (accessed on 17 August 2021).

Chapter 2

Harassment at Workplace: An Overview

CONTENTS

Harassment at the workplace refers to any unwelcome and offensive conduct from a boss, co-worker, vendor, or customer within the workspace. The current chapter proposes to shed light on the nature and dynamics of harassment at the workplace. It further discusses in detail the finer aspects of the subject, such as, its causes, types, and impacts. It also sheds light on the remedial action for its redressal and the strategies to be developed by an organization in order to prevent instances of harassment within the workspace and promote a healthy work culture.

2.1. INTRODUCTION

Workplace harassment is the belittling or threatening behavior directed at an individual worker or a group of workers. The issue of workplace harassment is a topic that has garnered much interest and attention amongst practitioners and researchers in recent times, and is bound to become one of the most sensitive areas of effective workplace management.

Harassment is a form of employment discrimination that violates Title VII of the Civil Rights Act of 1964, the Age Discrimination in Employment Act (ADEA) of 1967, and the Americans with Disabilities Act of 1990. Harassment is an unwelcome conduct that is based on race, color, religion, sex (including pregnancy), national origin, age (40 or older), disability, or genetic information (including family medical history).

Harassment becomes unlawful where (1) enduring the offensive conduct becomes a condition of continued employment, or (2) the conduct is severe or pervasive enough to create a work environment that a reasonable person would consider intimidating, hostile, or abusive.

Anti-discrimination laws also prohibit harassment against individuals in retaliation for filing a discrimination charge, testifying, or participating in any way in an investigation, proceeding, or lawsuit under these laws; or opposing employment practices that they reasonably believe discriminate against individuals, in violation of these laws.

Harassment often turns out to be an expensive affair for employers. Additionally, it has certain negative impacts such as low morale amongst employees, absenteeism, diminished productivity, employee turnover, and damages and litigation costs. The 2014 Workplace Bullying Institute, Zogby national survey, highlights that 27% have experienced workplace bullying in the past, and 7% of employees currently suffer workplace bullying. Workplace harassment is a critical issue that needs to be addressed with prompt action in order to reach a better scenario at the workplace. Data shows that a majority of the professionals who experience harassment, in some form or the other, are overtly reluctant to report the same due to numerous reasons, such as: the fear of losing the job and its disastrous consequences and facing the aftermath.

The development of a robust policy framework is essential to solve the problem of workplace harassment. Deeper research into this subject will enable organizations to develop strategies that will help build an employee-friendly, safe, and healthy workplace environment.

Therefore, it can be concluded that workplace harassment is a raging issue and is mostly left unexpressed by the employees due to the fear and stigma associated with the same. Research suggests that sensitization of employees about a healthy workspace and work culture could help raise awareness and act as a strong deterrent in the fight against workplace harassment.

Both institutions and organizations must uphold and reiterate the rules of conduct within the workplace environment in order to avoid such instances and prevent the trauma it entails. A healthy and conducive work culture also ensures maximum work output by all employees.

2.2. WHAT IS WORKPLACE HARASSMENT?

Generally, harassment at workplace is most often associated with the objectionable, defamatory, maligning, intimidating, bullying, or otherwise unsolicited behavior leveled at a particular individual on the basis of certain protected characteristics, such as: age, race, color, religion, nationality, sex, gender identity, pregnancy, sexual orientation, disability, genetic information.

Harassment involves an extensive broad range of behavioral display such as: it can include a range of verbal or physical behavior, including: intimidating or offensive jokes and innuendos, demeaning remarks, name-calling, offensive nicknames, or slurs, exclusion or victimization, offensive pictures, or objects, including pornographic images, bullying, leering, unwelcome, offensive, or intimidating phone calls, physical assaults, threats, and intimidation (Figure 2.1).

Figure 2.1. Harassment at workplace.

Source: Image by Wikimedia commons.

Workplace harassment typically entails a specific pattern of on-going behavior, but it can also occur due to a single incident in cases where it is known to have a deep and long-lasting effect on an individual. Harassment at work, under British law is defined as, "Unwanted conduct related to a relevant protected characteristic, which has the purpose or effect of violating an individual's dignity or creating an intimidating, hostile, degrading, humiliating or offensive environment for that individual."

Workplace harassment is a burning issue. Yet, it cannot be seen only from the point of view of business. It exists throughout all types of workplaces in the U.S. From workplace bullying to outright discrimination, it is important to understand workplace harassment so you can avoid hostile work environments in your small business.

That may mean holding yearly training sessions with employees to define things like racial harassment and workplace bullying. By creating a workplace harassment policy, you can take the necessary steps to create a safe working environment for all your employees.

While the most basic types of harassment are verbal and psychological, there are also more serious forms, such as physical and sexual harassment. All types of workplace harassment are illegal and not only affect an employee's productivity, comfort, and safety at work, but also put the organization in legal jeopardy.

It is often seen in instances of workplace harassment that while the victims feel and believe that it would be easy for them to identify and report an incident of harassment to the supervisor, the incident quite often, renders them to feel highly vulnerable and unsafe and thereby they mostly grapple with the circumstances, leaving them confused and distressed.

Chris Chancey, founder of Amplio Recruiting, said that many victims of workplace harassment do not report it out of fear, and others are unsure of what conduct constitutes harassment.

"Some behaviors, albeit making someone uncomfortable, can seem so harmless-there are no physical signs of abuse-that few people want to report them for fear of being seen as petty or as a snitch," Chancey told Business News Daily.

Since the issue of workplace harassment is a sensitive one, it has to be approached and handled in a careful and unbiased manner. Therefore, all harassment claims must be taken seriously and prompt and thorough action needs to be taken along with maintaining confidentiality.

"If you are being harassed or think you may be, but are too scared to go forward, educating yourself on the facts is a great way to gain confidence to stand up for yourself," said Becca Garvin, executive search consultant at Find Great People. "The sooner you act on it, the easier it will be to put an end to it."

Under federal law and Department of Labor (DOL) policy, harassment by DOL employees of DOL employees based on race, color, religion, sex (including gender identity and pregnancy), national origin, age, disability, genetic information, sexual orientation, or parental status is prohibited. The Department of Labor does not permit harassing conduct by anyone in the workplace, including contractors.

Prohibited workplace harassment generally takes place in two forms. It may entail "quid pro quo" harassment, which means something for something. It simply means that an individual is offered a certain employment benefit in return for accepting unwanted behavior from a supervisor.

It mostly occurs in cases in which employment decisions or treatment are subject to accepting or declining any form of unwarranted conduct, generally conduct of a sexual nature. It may also take place in instances wherein the employer hits back after their advances have been spurned off by an employee. Workplace harassment can also be non-sexual in nature. In such cases, demeaning, and objectionable conduct and behavior is carried out by the superior group and is found to be extremely acute and thereby results in a hostile or unfriendly workspace. It also occurs when an unfavorable choice is made by the employee such as being fired or demoted.

DOL policies and procedures promote instantaneous identification, recognition, reporting, and redressal of objectionable and harassing workplace conduct. The intent of these policies is to rectify and further eradicate such behavior and conduct even in instances wherein the said conduct was not harsh and ubiquitous that it be considered a transgression of a federal law.

As of January 1, 2021, changes to rules relating to workplace violence, harassment, and sexual harassment in federal workplaces have changed. Policies in the federal government's new Workplace Harassment and Violence Prevention Regulations, and corresponding changes to the Canada Labor Code have been consolidated and broadened in Part II of the Code.

The definition of workplace "violence and harassment" has been expanded to include: "Any action, conduct or comment, including of a sexual nature, that can reasonably be expected to cause offence, humiliation or other physical or psychological injury or illness to an employee."

2.2.1. What Constitutes Workplace Harassment?

Harassment at the workplace is often found to occur either with or without any material evidence or verification. Its authentication may not always be easy to verify or prove. When approaching the matter of harassment, it is necessary to fully understand the victim's point of view.

According to the Equal Employment Opportunity Commission (EEOC), misconduct can include offensive jokes, slurs, epithets or name-calling, physical assaults or threats, intimidation, ridicule or mockery, insults or put-downs, offensive objects or pictures, and interference with work performance.

Harassment also often occurs in a variety of circumstances, such as the following:

- The harasser could be the victim's supervisor, a supervisor in another area, an agent of the employer, a co-worker, or a nonemployee;

- The victim does not have to be the person harassed, but could be anyone affected by the offensive conduct;
- Unlawful harassment may occur without economic injury to or discharge of the victim.

First and foremost, Garvin said, it is critical to know when you are being harassed at work. Workplace harassment is a serious issue with a lot of gray areas. If you witness a crime or experience harassment in the workplace, it is your obligation to report it. If you are worried about losing your job in retaliation, remember that you are protected by workplace harassment laws.

"Not only are you protected [by law] from the person(s) harassing you, [but] you are also protected from your employer failing to protect you," Garvin said. "If you know someone who is being harassed at work, you cannot lose your job by reporting it yourself."

2.3. IDENTIFYING WORKPLACE HARASSMENT AND ITS DYNAMICS

Harassment in any form and of any degree is an absolute no-no at the workplace. An employer subject to federal anti-discrimination laws is legally obliged and compelled to maintain and make provision of a safe and healthy work environment, that is free from intimidation, insult, or ridicule based on race, color, religion, gender, or national origin. The employers must also ensure undertaking the necessary steps for minimizing and eliminating incidents of harassment in order to steer clear of being sued in state courts.

As an employer, it is possible to be held accountable for any act of harassment at workplaces, not just by the employer itself but also by any manager or employee, or even by customers, suppliers, and any other individual engaged in the business causing distress to the employees.

Harassment refers to verbal or physical conduct that belittles or displays bitterness or aversion toward an individual on account of that person's (or that person's relatives,' friends,' or associates') race, skin color, religion, gender, national origin, age, or disability, and that:

- has the purpose or effect of creating an intimidating, hostile, or offensive work environment;
- has the purpose or effect of unreasonably interfering with the individual's work performance;
- otherwise adversely affects the individual's employment opportunities.

Harassing conduct includes: epithets; slurs; negative stereotyping; or threatening, intimidating, or hostile acts that relate to race, color, religion, gender, national origin, age, or disability (including jokes or pranks that are hostile or demeaning with regard to race, color, religion, gender, national origin, age, or disability), written or graphic material that denigrates or shows hostility or aversion toward an individual or group because of race, color, religion, gender, national origin, age, or disability and that is displayed on walls, bulletin boards, or other locations on your premises or circulated in the workplace.

2.3.1. The Reasonable Person Standard

In a situation where an employer is trying to ascertain and comprehend whether or not a particular behavior or conduct fits the definition of harassing conduct, it is utmost crucial to decide it by deploying the "reasonable person" standard. This simply means that if a reasonable, rational, and unbiased person in a similar situation would define the conduct as intimidating, hostile, or abusive, then it is most likely that it is a standard case of harassment.

The reasonable person standard is a technique that takes into consideration the viewpoint and outlook of persons of the same race, color, religion, gender, national origin, age, or disability as the harassment victim. For instance, in the case of a black woman complaining of harassment with a racial undertone, it is necessary to take into account the perspective of a black woman, and not a white woman or man. In doing so, if the perspective of the other woman is similar to that of the victim, the conduct can be deemed as harassing conduct.

Irrespective of the fact that in the judgement of any conduct of harassment, it is critical to do so impartially and without any form of prejudice, yet, it is necessary to uphold the subjective perception of the harassed employee in question. In cases where the employee does not believe or affirm to the work environment to be contentious and hostile, it is safe to assume that the conduct or behavior in question does not qualify as unlawful harassment.

2.3.2. Example

In a situation, where let us assume, there are six co-workers, five male and one female, telling "blonde jokes," and none of the employees finds them offensive, hostile, or abusive, the conduct is not harassment. However, it is always safer to alert the employees with respect to their behavior and the potential risk of it being viewed as a form of verbal and mental harassment.

2.4. WHY DOES IT OCCUR?

The ground-breaking "Me Too" movement has sparked much debate worldwide about harassment at workplace and has opened a barrage of unspoken voices lending support and strength to thousands of people worldwide to come out and openly speak up about their trials and tribulations while facing unjust and offensive conduct at the workplace.

However, not every individual who experiences workplace harassment is able to gather courage and speak up about it. Countless victims have dubious thoughts and are wary of complaining and reporting harassing behaviors of either fellow colleagues or managers.

Workplace harassment is a rampant malpractice and though it is a recurring phenomenon at any given workspace, yet it is not openly discussed. Harassment at work leads to a toxic and threatening workplace. Due to ignorance and being ill-informed, numerous individuals are unaware of the dynamics and nature of harassment at work which tragically results in most cases of harassment going ignored, unreported, and unidentified. Many times, due to confrontational and unfriendly work environments, many employees often quit their jobs and organizations.

Every day, employees are abused and bullied at work. In fact, the issue of workplace bullying affects nearly one-fifth of all employees at some point during their careers or 60.3 million Americans every year, according to the Workplace Bullying Institute.

The following are some of the most common reasons for the occurrence of workplace harassment and they tend to explain the reason behind people falling prey to workplace bullies.

2.4.1. Targets Are Skilled Workers

It is very likely that as a result of being likable and well-appreciated, an employee might encounter being bullied or harassed at work. It is often witnessed at workspaces, that employees who are intelligent, go-getters, those who think-out-of-the-box and are lauded for their constant contribution of new and innovative ideas and those who go the extra mile and are showered with admiration recognition for their diligence and hard work are often the main targets of workplace bullies (Figure 2.2).

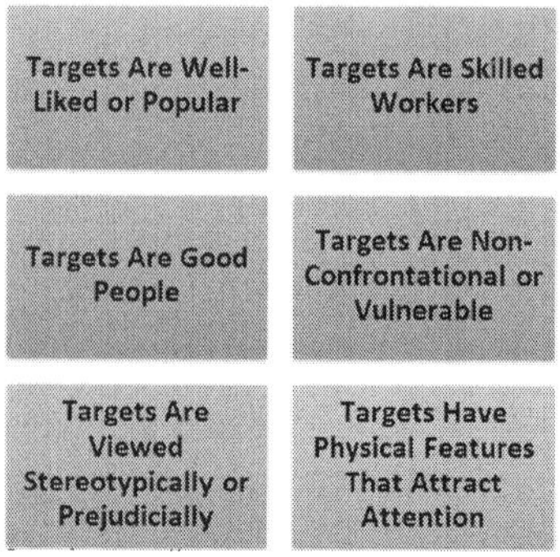

Figure 2.2. Reasons of occurring sexual harassment.

While these employees succeed and finish projects, there are others who are struggling to cope with the pressures of office work. This leads to a certain sense of inferiority amongst the bullies and seeing their hard work being overlooked due to the abilities and achievements of another employee, they target such people at work.

A classic example of this scenario is when bullying bosses pick and choose extremely skilled workers with the intention of hogging the limelight as a result of the target's hard work or in certain circumstances to sabotage the target's efforts.

2.4.2. Targets Are Well-Liked or Popular

It is often assumed that those who are bullied or harassed at the workplace are either loners or introverts with low social skills and no friends or social circle. On the contrary, it is commonly seen that the most sought-after and well-known employees fall prey to workplace bullying. Bullies at the workplace, view such people as a major threat to their own popularity and social status at work. Therefore, in order to bring such people down, bullies often form a coterie or an 'inner circle' and make constant attacks on the targets.

2.4.3. Targets Are Good People

It is often found that compassionate, social, and collaborative people are subject to workplace harassment. To a workplace bully, these characteristics drain the power they have. As opposed to the target, bullies are not in favor of team work and mostly wish to hog all the attention and appreciation by themselves. Therefore, often people who are strong team players are often subject to bullying and harassment.

Targets are often noted for their ethics and principles. They could be harmed for their honesty and loyalty. For instance, whistle-blowers who blow the lid off major scams and frauds are constantly bullied and troubled at work with the intention of keeping them quiet in an attempt to cover up the malpractices.

2.4.4. Targets Are Non-Confrontational or Vulnerable

Studies have found that shy, introverted, anxious, or passively obedient employees are more prone to being bullied at work than those who are extroverted, opinionated, and assertive. Research suggests that those adults who work on their self-esteem and build a confidence level and are assertive and forthright eliminate their chances to a minimum of being targeted by workplace bullies. In certain specific cases, certain theories suggest that depression, anxiety, and other stress-related issues cause employees to be more vulnerable to bullying.

2.4.5. Targets Are Viewed Stereotypically or Prejudicially

In simpler terms, an employee is likely to be targeted because of their gender, age, race, sexual preference, or religion. Targets could also face bullying due to any disability or a disease. Most often, irrespective of the reason, bullies at the workplace, target employees who are different from the majority on some account or the other. It also leads to discrimination at workplace.

2.4.6. Targets Have Physical Features That Attract Attention

As is seen in high schools, kids target each other on the basis of their different appearance, bullies at the workplace, too, often find similar reasons to target fellow employees. Being tall, short, fat, thin, having a certain accent, facial features, could all work against the targets as the workplace bullies engage in small talk and make rude comments to humiliate others based on their appearance and personality.

As a matter of fact, almost any basic physical trait could be used as a weapon to mock the physical appearance of the target. This includes wearing glasses, having a large nose, having ears that protrude, and even having adult acne.

The human resources (HRs) or manpower of any organization is its biggest asset and the key to its success. A hostile and unfair workplace and work environment will not yield maximum productivity of all employees as it will have serious implications on the employee's health and mental and emotional well-being. It will also damage employee relations and the brand value and the organization's reputation in the world of business.

Therefore, it is necessary to strictly follow and practice a policy of zero tolerance towards harassment and thereby ensure a safe and healthy work environment for reaping the maximum benefit out of the business by offering a conducive and just work environment.

Harassment at the workplace has been found to be one of the foremost reasons of stress and mental injury, with particular patterns and consequences for marginalized workers. Oppression is a root cause of harassment. Marginalized workers are gravely impacted, yet almost all workers suffer to some extent or the other.

Often the plight of marginalized workers is attributed to the poor and inhumane working conditions offered to them. Privatization is another factor that is additionally increasing this burden on them. In order to diminish these situations, far-reaching, and concrete solutions need to be formed.

Harassment is a significant occupational hazard. It has direct implications on the physical and psychological safety, and it jeopardizes their chances of safety from other additional work hazards. Harassment is one of the main types of workplace stressors.

Workers who suffer being marginalized on accounts of sexism, misogyny, homophobia, trans phobia, racism, colonialism, albinism, and other forms of oppression are often found at the brink of workplace harassment hazards and effects and experience a different form of harassment in comparison to other workers. The exposures and impacts that these hazards have on marginalized workers too vary from one individual to the other.

Understaffing, job insecurity and other poor working conditions are the major forms of harassment whereas organizational restructuring, pay-cuts, and privatization are further aggravating the existing conditions. Marginalized groups are the group that are found to suffer most due to these alterations, as workers and as users/clients.

Oppression causes major damage to all workers, not just marginalized workers. It severely pollutes the work environment and causes irreversible damage in spite of reduced or completely eliminated incidents of harassment.

In order to eradicate all forms of persecution, maltreatment, suppression, and organizationally-driven harassment, strong, and legally enforceable rights that tend to address the very core of these problems must be formulated.

A rather popular view is that these types of behaviors are deeply rooted within the personality structure of the office or shop-floor bully. However, not much empirical evidence exists for this notion. Yet, in one study we did find that self-reported bullies described themselves as being high on aggressiveness and low on self-esteem, the latter being particularly true for a group of offenders who also saw themselves as a target of bullying (Matthiesen and Einarsen, 2005). These perpetrators, labeled as provocative targets, were also found to be low on social competence and high on social anxiety.

A controversial issue in this research is the role of the victim personality. Studies indicate that such factors may in fact play a role, at least in the victimization process resulting from exposure to bullying behaviors in the workplace, and at least in some of the cases.

A study of personality and personality disorders among 85 Norwegian victims of bullying at work using a comprehensive measure of personality called the MMPI-2 revealed some interesting insights (Matthiesen and Einarsen, 2001).

As a group, victims portrayed a personality profile indicating a tendency to emotional and psychological disturbance on a wide range of personality factors. However, the study showed that victims of bullying were not a homogeneous group. One group of victims portrayed a profile indicating an extreme range of severe psychological problems and personality disturbances.

This group, called the "seriously affected," reported a range of emotional and psychological problems although they reported a relatively low exposure to specific bullying behaviors, a finding indicating that personality is important in determining how bullying is experienced and how it is reacted to.

These victims were depressed, anxious, suspicious, uncertain of themselves, and troubled by confused thoughts. A second group, called the "disappointed and depressed" portrayed a tendency towards becoming depressed and being suspicious of the outside world. The third group, called the "common group," portrayed a quite normal personality, in spite of having experienced the largest number of specific bullying behaviors.

Such results may indicate that a specific vulnerability/hardiness factor may exist among some but not all victims of bullying at work. Persons who are already suffering from psychological problems are probably more likely to suffer long-term psychological and physical problems in the wake of bullying and serious personal conflicts. Persons with psychological problems, low self-confidence, and a high degree of anxiety in social situations may also be more likely than others to feel bullied and harassed, and they may find it more difficult to defend them if they are exposed to the aggression of other people.

However, a caution must be put forward. Interviews with victims as well as case studies (Einarsen et al., 1994) reveal that bullying seems to exist only in organizational cultures that permit or reward such kinds of behavior (see also Einarsen et al., 2003).

Bullying will only take place if the offender feels he or she has the blessing, support, or at least the implicit permission of his superiors to behave in this manner (Brodsky, 1976). In some organizations, bullying may even be institutionalized as a part of leadership and managerial practice.

Authoritarian leadership styles are still highly valued in many companies (Hoel and Salin, 2003). Blaming it all on the "psychopaths at work" or even a "neurotic" victim is therefore in most cases a too simplistic solution to the problem of why bullying takes place.

In addition to the values and norms prevailing in the organizational culture, the quality of the psychosocial work environment seems to be an important cause of bullying. A work situation characterized by role conflict and a lack of interesting and challenging work tasks, combined with a negative interpersonal climate in the work group, seems to be a high-risk situation for bullying (Einarsen et al., 1996).

A high degree of ambiguity or incompatible demands and expectations about roles, tasks, and responsibilities may create a high degree of frustration and conflicts within the work group, especially in connection with rights, obligations, privileges, and positions. This situation may then act as a precursor of conflict, poor inter-worker relationships, and a need for a suitable scapegoat, especially if the social climate is characterized by low trust and interpersonal tension.

A typical characteristic of workplaces where bullying prevails is also low satisfaction among many employees regarding the leadership style of their managers and supervisors; it is either too aggressive or too laissez-faire. In fact, as many as 50% of bullying victims claim to be bullied by a superior, again linking bullying closely to leadership. These findings can be summarized by Leymann's (1993) theoretical claim that four factors are prominent in eliciting bullying at work:

- a deficiency in work design;
- a deficiency in leadership behavior;
- a socially exposed position of the victim; and
- a low moral standard in the department.

2.5. CONSEQUENCES OF WORKPLACE HARASSMENT

There could be serious consequences of harassment for anybody who is involved in it, including those who witness the harassment, the victim, and people who are impacted emotionally through it, and the employer as well. Harassment in the workplace is an on-going risk to the safety of the employees and the business. The consequences of harassment in the workplace have a far-reaching impression on everything from the company's bottom line, to employee morale, and to the reputation of an individual as well.

A 2007 Zogby International survey found that 37% of workers-approximately 54 million people-reported bullying at work. Irrespective of its nature or degree, harassment in all forms at a workplace is hazardous and unacceptable.

From bullying to discrimination on the basis of sex, race or other legally protected characteristics, all forms of harassment create a toxic and passively hostile work environment that poses as a serious threat to the reputation of an organization and also bears significant trauma on the victim hampering their emotional and psychological well-being and lowering their productivity and efficiency (Figure 2.3).

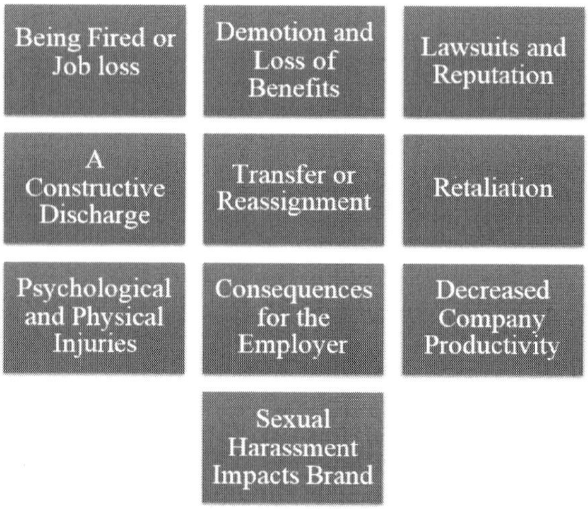

Figure 2.3. Consequences of workplace harassment.

Talking about any workplace, there are several possible results of the harassment. Out of which, some may be less obvious as compared to the others, but no less damaging, here is the list of it.

2.5.1. Being Fired or Job Loss

Every so often, there is a clear connection between the harassment and the harm done by it. There is a possibility that one may be fired or demoted for refusing the sexual overtures of a colleague or supervisor. Sometimes, an individual will be given some wrong explanation for being fired, but the real reason remains very clear.

Even if there is a legal or valid explanation for an individual to be fired, the decision to do so may still be connected to the harassment. For instance, if the upper management demotes an individual, and the reason behind that is a person complained about the harassment, then, there could be a possibility he or she fires that person for objecting to the demotion, but still the root cause will be the harassment.

In the same manner, if a person is incompetent to work for an interval of time because of the harassment and the upper management or the manager uses this as a reason to fire that person, the firing is still an outcome of the harassment.

2.5.2. A Constructive Discharge

Every so often, the harassment is so unbearable that the victim quits their job even before they are fired. In a case when the harassment is so severe that it validates the victim leaving the job, it will be well-thought out as a constructive discharge.

In simple words, the victim was forced out of a job and the reason behind this will be harassment. Nevertheless, this can be very difficult to prove, generally, the courts will consider the victim to have been unlawfully fired.

For instance, if a person works for an organization or a firm where he or she is regularly imperiled to sexual advances from the boss, which, in the end, will lead the boss or the manager to giving that person the ultimatum, "Sleep with me or get fired!," the court will likely rule that the combination of the routine sexual advances, the ultimatum, as well as the danger of being fired made the situation so unbearable that any reasonable person would feel forced to quit the job, which will constitute a constructive discharge.

2.5.3. Demotion and Loss of Benefits

An individual may also be denied a promotion or be demoted when, for instance, a person refuses an upper management executive or co-workers sexual advances. This can lead that person to also losing the standing in the company, which can endanger the pay increments, promotions, and employment opportunities in future.

Generally, a demotion is accompanied by the loss of other employment benefits, for example:

- Wages;
- Pension contributions;
- Medical benefits;
- Overtime pays;
- Sick pay;
- Bonuses;
- Vacation pays;
- Profit sharing contributions.

2.5.4. A Transfer or Reassignment

Now and then, an employee who complains about the harassment, eventually he or she will be re-assigned or transferred to the other branch, or location or department, within the company. On the other hand, the harasser goes scot-free. In many scenarios, being reassigned or being transferred can be well-thought out as a punishment for taking stand about the harassment, more particularly if its outcome is in the form of loss of any pay, loss of any benefits, or loss of any opportunities for advancement in future.

2.5.5. Retaliation

Nevertheless, contrary to both state laws as well as federal laws, the victims of harassment are sometimes suspended, reproached, or otherwise fined for filing a complaint about the harassment. This is referred to as retaliation and it is considered as an actionable harm which is resulting from the harassment. In simple words, retaliation can lead to a lawsuit being filed against the employer by the person who files the complaint about the harassment.

2.5.6. Psychological and Physical Injuries

Along with the consequences that are related to employment, the victims of harassment often suffer from harassment-related psychological wounds or damages as well, which could consist of lowered self-esteem, depression, sleep disorders, anxiety, headaches, weight loss or gain, and sexual dysfunction. But, on the other hand, the psychological as well as the emotional injuries are more common, pranks, and violent acts perpetrated against the victim can also result in them suffering physical injuries, for example, cut, and lacerations, or broken bones.

Sexual harassment can also cause havoc on the performance of the job and career trajectory of a victim. Fear and decrement in confidence can cause some people to withdraw from the workplace and disengage from colleagues and associates. Victims of harassment are more likely to be neglecting duties, tardy, distracted, and absent.

If the victims of sexual harassment files a complaint of the harassment, they may suffer the advancement setbacks for example, being passed over for promotions, being left out of keys meetings, retaliation, and being labeled as a troublemaker. Issues related to finances such as lost wages and unpaid leave are also possible.

2.5.7. Consequences for the Employer

Beyond the consequences it can have for the victims and those who have witnessed the harassment, workplace harassment can have a direct impact on the employer with respect to the increased absenteeism, higher employee turnover, loss of morale, lower productivity, and the cost of fighting harassment lawsuits, all of which can add up to millions of dollars.

2.5.8. Decreased Company Productivity

Sexual harassment cause damage to a company or firm as well. When an office or workplace is infected with the discrimination and harassment, it causes disturbance to everyone. The hostility created by the harassment roots animosity, stress, low morale, absenteeism, gossip, and anxiety between the associates or colleagues.

Low productivity is more common in these sorts of environments which are having high rates of sexual harassment. Victims and witnesses of sexual harassment are more likely to resign or quit the job, which leads to high employee turnover and related hiring and training cost increases. A toxic environment will also make recruiting top talent more difficult.

2.5.9. Lawsuits and Reputation

A company's failure to effectively stop and handle the sexual harassment can outcome as in expensive lawsuits. In the time period of last 10 years, it has been observed that, some eye-popping jury awards in sexual harassment cases.

For example, a jury awarded plaintiffs $17.4 million in a case filed by the EEOC which was involved in rape and sexual harassment by three male supervisors at a Florida packing plant. And $18 million has been awarded in a case against a New York Global Group CEO (Chief Executive Officer) for retaliation against his former employee after she refused his advances. A highly publicized case of sexual harassment can also damage a company's reputation, resulting lost business.

In 2019, it was reported that the U.S. EEOC received over 7,514 claims of sexual harassment, resulting in $68 million in direct settlements.

2.5.10. Sexual Harassment Impacts Brand

Research has consistently suggested that once end consumers are informed about any incident of "incivility" towards an employee within the workplace, a very strong negative connotation is formed and associated with the firm involved resulting in loss of potential customer base. The brand value is majorly hit by news highlighting instances of harassment of employees.

Surveys have shown that employees who have experienced an unfair and biased work environment or some degree of harassment actively engage in negative publicity of the organization, product or service involved and thereby, demotivate potential buyers or customers to be associated with their employer.

2.6. REMEDIES FOR WORKPLACE HARASSMENT

In instances of discrimination, the motive of the law is to ensure that the victim who has suffered discrimination is elevated back to the position that he or she would have been at had the incident of discrimination never taken place.

The kind of relief offered to the victim will be decided according to the discriminatory action faced by the victim and the degree to which it has impacted the victim. For instance, in a case when a particular individual is rejected for a job or a promotion on the basis of some discrimination, the remedial solution may be an offer to the same job or position applied for and/or back pay and benefits the person would have received.

The employer would further be asked to ensure the removal of any other form of discriminatory practices and undertake all the necessary action to eliminate the chances of any sort of discrimination in the future.

A victim of discrimination might also be offered a full recovery of the attorney's fees, expert witness fees, and other additional court costs incurred during the procedure. Furthermore, remedies might also include "Compensatory and Punitive Damages."

Compensatory and punitive damages may be awarded in cases involving intentional discrimination based on a person's race, color, national origin, sex (including pregnancy, gender identity, and sexual orientation), religion, disability, or genetic information.

Compensatory damages pay victims for out-of-pocket expenses caused by the discrimination (such as costs associated with a job search or medical expenses) and compensate them for any emotional harm suffered (such as mental anguish, inconvenience, or loss of enjoyment of life).

Punitive damages are generally awarded to punish an employer who has committed an exceptionally spiteful, rash, and careless act of discrimination.

2.6.1. Limits on Compensatory and Punitive Damages

There are limits on the amount of compensatory and punitive damages a person can recover. These limits vary depending on the size of the employer:

For employers with 15–100 employees, the limit is $50,000.

For employers with 101–200 employees, the limit is $100,000.

For employers with 201–500 employees, the limit is $200,000.

For employers with more than 500 employees, the limit is $300,000.

2.6.2. Age or Sex Discrimination and Liquidated Damages

In cases involving intentional age discrimination, or in cases involving intentional sex-based wage discrimination under the Equal Pay Act, victims cannot recover either compensatory or punitive damages, but may be entitled to "liquidated damages."

Liquidated damages may be awarded to punish a specifically vindictive or reckless act of discrimination. The amount of liquidated damages that may be awarded is equal to the amount of back pay awarded to the victim.

In addition to what an employer can/should do to respond to harassment in the workplace, it is also important to understand the types of damages ("remedies" or "relief") that can be awarded in litigation against an employer where illegal harassment is proven. As a starting place, the federal EEOC and most state agencies are authorized to seek broad relief on behalf of aggrieved employees.

The relief may include, for example, compensation for lost wages and benefits, front pay, compensatory damages, hiring, reinstatement or promotion, fines, or mandatory changes in an employer's policies or practices. And this is just a partial list. If a plaintiff proves that an employer retaliated against an employee for reporting harassment or participating in harassment investigations, the scope of the possible remedies is even broader.

Under Title VII of the Civil Rights Act of 1964, a federal antidiscrimination law that applies to most private employers, the damages awards were generally limited to back pay and injunctive relief (such as an order requiring an employer to cease and desist from continuing an unlawful practice).

Compensatory damages and punitive damages generally were not available. With the passage of the Civil Rights Act of 1991 (CRA) came an expansion of remedies that was designed to meet the twin goals of the law:

to deter discrimination and harassment and to compensate the victim. Under Title VII, as amended by the CRA, the remedies available (as of January 2006) may include:

- Back pay;
- Hiring, promotion, or reinstatement;
- Front pay.

Other actions that will make the victim "whole" (put the victim in the condition he/she would have been in but for the discrimination). An award of attorneys' fees, expert witness fees, and/or court costs. Injunctive relief ordering that certain conduct be stopped or requiring changes to policies or practices. Compensatory damages for future pecuniary loss, emotional pain and suffering, mental anguish, and other non-pecuniary losses. Under the CRA, compensatory, and punitive damages are subject to certain maximum amounts ("caps"), based on the size of the employer.

The remedies under most states' discrimination laws are just as broad as federal law and, in some cases, provide additional relief. For example, under the Fair Employment and Housing Act in California, an employee who has been discriminated against or harassed is entitled to compensatory damages (including damages for emotional distress), punitive damages, attorneys' fees, and expert witness fees.

Specifically, the possible remedies for employment discrimination in California include:

- Back pay;
- Hiring, promotion, or reinstatement;
- Out-of-pocket expenses;
- Front pay;
- Injunctive relief ordering that certain conduct be stopped or requiring changes to policies or practices;
- Imposition of additional training requirements;
- Actual and compensatory damages for future pecuniary loss, emotional pain and suffering, mental anguish, and other non-pecuniary losses;
- An award of attorneys' fees, expert witness fees, and/or court costs;
- Punitive damages.

Additionally, at the agency stage of the complaint process, many states' laws authorize the agency that is charged with enforcing the employment discrimination laws to impose administrative fines against private employers. The amount of the fines will vary by state but can be as high as treble (triple) damages.

For example, in California (as of January 2006), the fines are combined with any damages awarded for emotional distress and cannot exceed $150,000 per aggrieved person per employer. And if the individual pursues his or her case in a private lawsuit against the employer, the remedies are identical to the relief the agency can get, with two important exceptions: there is no limit on the amount of emotional distress damages, and unlimited punitive damages may be awarded instead of administrative fines.

The relief awarded to a plaintiff can also be expanded further than the limit that is demarcated and authorized under the discrimination laws. This is so, because numerous lawsuits that are allegedly pursued in the pretext of harassment or discrimination are also found to be furnished with additional claims against the employer, with each claim adding additional remedies.

For instance, in a case that is being fought on grounds of harassment, it is quite possible, for the plaintiff to include separately stated claims for intentional infliction of emotional distress, assault, battery, false imprisonment, violation of the right to privacy, defamation, etc. although, it is not necessary that the plaintiff will experience triumph over all the claims alleged, it only takes success in one of them for there to be a broader right to recover damages not subject to any limitations that may apply under specific discrimination laws.

In such cases, the likely expense incurred by the employers if found guilty of discrimination or harassment can be exorbitant. Additionally, the other costs incurred throughout the process, i.e., the non-monetary costs (such as injury to reputation, low employee morale, loss of valuable employees and/ or clients, time spent defending against the cases, decrease in productivity, etc.), it can be easily assumed that the actual costs can never be estimated.

Consequently, the prevention and complete expulsion of all sorts of harassment and discriminatory practices is the finest solution for both the employer and the employee. The formation and sustainability of a work space free from all forms of prejudice and built on trust, mutual respect and uniform treatment is the best remedy to workplace harassment.

2.7. GLOBAL OVERVIEW OF HARASSMENT

Establishing a world where all work is free from any sort of discrimination or bias is central to the idea of establishing a just workplace. The principles of non-discrimination and equality are recognized internationally as central to any system of human rights protection and embedded in most countries 'constitutions and in human rights treaties. In the world of work, non-discrimination, and equal opportunity and treatment are considered to be basic human and labor rights, fundamental for social justice and sustainable development.

The ILO Declaration of Philadelphia of 1944 affirms that all human beings, irrespective of race, creed, or sex, have the right to pursue both their material well-being and their spiritual development in conditions of freedom and dignity, of economic security and equal opportunity, and that discrimination constitutes a violation of rights enunciated by the Universal Declaration of Human Rights (UDHR).

About 15 years after the adoption of the ILO Declaration of Philadelphia, ILO member States adopted the Discrimination (Employment and Occupation) Convention, 1958 (No. 111) in 1958. This Convention aims to protect all persons against discrimination at work, and requires ratifying States to ensure protection against discrimination in employment and occupation on seven grounds, namely race, color, sex, religion, political opinion, national extraction, and social origin, as well as other grounds prohibited in national legislation by governments after consultation with the representative employers' and workers' organizations.

Convention No. 111 belongs to the fundamental ILO Conventions, and it is the most comprehensive international instrument dedicated to guide national legislation on the promotion of non-discrimination and equality in the world of work.

The principles of non-discrimination and equality in workplaces are widely accepted and the Convention has been ratified by 172 member States including India, thereby expressing their commitments to uphold the human rights of workers and progressively incorporate equality and non-discrimination principles in the world of work and other laws and regulations.

Despite the international consensus and commitment at national level to eliminate discrimination and to promote equality of opportunity and treatment, various forms of discrimination continue to prevail in the world of work preventing women and men to enjoy decent work.

One form of discrimination on the ground of sex that should be addressed within the requirement of the Convention is sexual harassment. Sexual harassment can be perpetuated against both women and men. However, the majority of cases of sexual harassment in the workplace are perpetuated by men against women as women often do not have equal status as men, lack power, and are in more vulnerable and insecure positions.

While it is difficult to quantify the prevalence of sexual harassment in the workplace due to the varying definitions and perceptions of sexual harassment and reluctance of the harassed to report their experiences, studies have revealed that sexual harassment at workplace is a reality for a large number of women.

In Australia, the results of a national telephone survey in 2012 by the Australian Human Rights Commission showed that sexual harassment in workplaces in the country was widespread. It showed that there were approximately one in five people aged 15 years and older who were sexually harassed in the workplace in the past five years; one in four women (25%) and one in six men (16%) have been sexually harassed in the workplace in the past five years.

Targets of sexual harassment were found to be mostly women under 40 years of age, and harassers were mostly male co-workers. The survey also indicated that women are at least five times more likely than men to have been harassed by a boss or employer. Men harassing women accounted for more than half of all sexual harassment, while male harassment of men accounted for nearly a quarter.

In European Union (EU) countries, between 40 and 50% of women experience unwanted sexual advances, physical contact, or other forms of sexual harassment at work. In the United States (U.S.), 83% of girls aged 12 to 16 experienced some form of sexual harassment in public schools. Across Asia, studies in Japan, Malaysia, the Philippines, and South Korea showed that 30 to 40% of women suffer workplace sexual harassment.

2.8. CONCLUSION

Harassment of any kind or degree has no place in a safe and neutral work environment. Workplace harassment occurs when an employee or a group of employees feel threatened or are humiliated within their workspace by their colleagues or superiors. The main intention of a harasser at a workplace is to jeopardize the physical, emotional, and mental well-being of the victim and create a hurdle in their professional career. Harassment encompasses numerous types of classifications and is not subjected upon any specific target group. On the contrary, harassment occurs when people get together and target multiple groups such as women, minority racial groups, sexual minorities, people suffering from disabilities and immigrants.

The implications of harassment widely range from hampered brand value to lawsuits and from being fired to infliction of severe physical and psychological trauma. Workplace harassment is a discriminatory prototype of behavior that builds a hostile environment ensuring protection to the perpetrators.

Therefore, the foremost and safest tool to eradicate the evil of workplace harassment is preventive measures. Employers should be positively motivated to undertake necessary action to prevent and rectify unlawful harassment.

A clear communication channel should be formed between the employer and the employee ensuring that all incidents of unwelcome harassing conduct are reported. An effective and transparent complaint or grievance process must be established and provision of anti-harassment training must be made to their managers and employees.

This will ensure swift and suitable action and take immediate and appropriate action when an employee complains. Employers should endeavor to create a friendly and safe work environment where all employees feel safe and exercise their freedom to openly raise attention to issues and concerns of harassment and have their concerns addressed.

Therefore, employers need to formulate anti-harassment programs that help give way for establishing a positive work culture free from harassment of any form. Employers must hold employees, and themselves, to high standards. All employees deserve to work in a workplace that is free from harassment and discrimination of any kind in order to increase productivity and maintain decorum.

A company's anti-harassment policy therefore, must establish an effective complaint procedure and encourage employees to feel comfortable coming to you with any problems they face at work, including any harassment that might occur.

It should also look into complaints on an immediate basis and undertake a full investigation of such incidents. Necessary documentation and an unbiased investigation are the key to addressing complaints of harassment at the workplace. Therefore, a safe and healthy work culture is possible only with a well-formulated and efficiently practiced policy at the workplace. Both of these solutions will act as major deterrents and help formulate better policies and safeguard all employees within the workspace from harassment.

REFERENCES

1. Amy, M., (2020). Six Reasons Why People are Bullied at Work. [Online] Verywell Mind. Available at: https://www.verywellmind.com/reasons-why-workplace-bu (accessed on 17 August 2021).
2. Barrie, G., (2021). Legal Remedies for Harassment in the Workplace. [Online] AllBusiness.com. Available at: https://www.allbusiness.com/legal-remedies-for-harassment-in-the-workplace-12470-1.html (accessed on 17 August 2021).
3. Block, W., & Whitehead, R., (2019). Sexual harassment in the workplace. Palgrave Studies in Classical Liberalism, [Online] pp. 139–181. Available at: https://link.springer.com/chapter/10.1007%2F978-3-030-28360-5_5 (accessed on 17 August 2021).
4. Bright, H. R., (2021). Harassment the Workplace | BrightHR. [Online] Brighthr.com. Available at: https://www.brighthr.com/articles/equality-and-discrimination/harassment-at-work/ (accessed on 17 August 2021).
5. Brown, J., Drury, L., Raub, K., Levy, B., Brantner, P., Krivak, T., & Naumann, R., (2019). Workplace and sexual harassment and discrimination in gynecology. Gynecologic Oncology, [Online] 154, p. 10. Available at: https://www.gynecologiconcology-online.net/article/S0090-8258(19)30529-3/fulltext (accessed on 17 August 2021).
6. Creaser, F., (2020). Sexual harassment, pregnancy discrimination, and power harassment. Foreign Female English Teachers in Japanese Higher Education: Narratives from Our Quarter, [Online] pp. 267–282. Available at: https://www.researchgate.net/publication/346506529_Sexual_harassment_pregnancy_discrimination_and_power_harassment (accessed on 17 August 2021).
7. Crone Law Firm, (2021). What are the Consequences of Harassment? -The Crone Law Firm. [Online] The Crone Law Firm. Available at: https://cronelawfirmplc.com/blog/sexual-harassment/what-are-the-consequences-of-harassment/ (accessed on 17 August 2021).
8. Dean, E., (2018). Sexual harassment in the workplace. Emergency Nurse, [Online] 25(09), pp. 13. Available at: https://journals.rcni.com/emergency-nurse/sexual-harassment-in-the-workplace-en.25.09.13.s13 (accessed on 17 August 2021).
9. Dean, E., (2018). Sexual harassment in the workplace. Mental Health Practice, [Online] 21(05), pp. 10. Available at: https://journals.rcni.

com/mental-health-practice/sexual-harassment-in-the-workplace-mhp.21.05.10.s8 (accessed on 17 August 2021).

10. Einarsen, S., (2005). The nature, causes, and consequences of bullying at work: The Norwegian experience. Perspectives Interdisciplinaires sur le travail et la Santé, [Online]. Available at: https://journals.openedition.org/pistes/3156#tocto1n4 (accessed on 17 August 2021).
11. Girgis, C., (2020). Sexual harassment. Burnout in Women Physicians, [Online] pp. 105–128. Available at: https://link.springer.com/chapter/10.1007%2F978-3-030-44459-4_6 (accessed on 17 August 2021).
12. Gulseren, D., & Kelloway, E., (2019). Workplace: Sexual harassment. Encyclopedia of Security and Emergency Management, [Online] pp. 1–5. Available at: https://www.researchgate.net/publication/348402262_Workplace_Sexual_Harassment_Sexual_Harassment_in_the_Workplace (accessed on 17 August 2021).
13. Gustin, J., (2020). Sexual harassment. Workplace Violence and the Facility Manager, [Online] pp. 143–157. Available at: https://www.taylorfrancis.com/chapters/mono/10.1201/9781003151210-9/sexual-harassment-joseph-gustin (accessed on 17 August 2021).
14. Hatch-Maillette, M., & Scalora, M., (2002). Gender, sexual harassment, workplace violence, and risk assessment. Aggression and Violent Behavior, [Online] 7(3), pp. 271–291. Available at: https://www.sciencedirect.com/science/article/abs/pii/S135917890100043X?via%3Dihub (accessed on 17 August 2021).
15. Hope, A., & Munro, C., (2021). Getting to zero sexual harassment in the workplace. American Journal of Critical Care, [Online] 30(4), pp. 250–252. Available at: https://aacnjournals.org/ajcconline/article/30/4/250/31488/Getting-to-Zero-Sexual-Harassment-in-the-Workplace (accessed on 17 August 2021).
16. Imtiyaz, S., (2021). Sexual harassment at workplace. SSRN Electronic Journal, [Online] Available at: https://papers.ssrn.com/sol3/papers.cfm?abstract_id=3873900 (accessed on 17 August 2021).
17. Legal Line, (2021). What is Workplace Harassment? [Online] Legal line. Available at: https://www.legalline.ca/legal-answers/what-is-workplace-harassment/ (accessed on 17 August 2021).
18. Levett, L., (2015). Sexual harassment. The Encyclopedia of Clinical Psychology, [Online] pp. 1–3. Available at: https://onlinelibrary.wiley.

com/doi/10.1002/9781118625392.wbecp391 (accessed on 17 August 2021).

19. Lockhart, L., (2016). Sexual harassment in the workplace. Nursing Made Incredibly Easy! [Online] 14(6), pp. 55. Available at: https://journals.lww.com/nursingmadeincrediblyeasy/Fulltext/2016/11000/Sexual_harassment_in_the_workplace.13.aspx (accessed on 17 August 2021).
20. McDonald, P., & Charlesworth, S., (2015). Workplace sexual harassment at the margins. Work, Employment, and Society, [Online] 30(1), pp. 118–134. Available at: https://journals.sagepub.com/doi/10.1177/0950017014564615 (accessed on 17 August 2021).
21. Sahai, S., Goel, R., & Punni, M., (2020). Behavioral and emotional dimensions of sexual harassment at workplace. Emotion and Information Processing, [Online] pp. 79–95. Available at: https://link.springer.com/chapter/10.1007%2F978-3-030-48849-9_6 (accessed on 17 August 2021).
22. Sharma, D., (2016). Sexual harassment at workplace: Revisited. LBS Journal of Management and Research, [Online] 14(1), p. 53. Available at: http://www.indianjournals.com/ijor.aspx?target=ijor:lbsjmr&volume=14&issue=1&article=005 (accessed on 17 August 2021).
23. Shrestha, N., (2013). Workplace sexual harassment in hospitals. Journal of Kathmandu Medical College, [Online] 1(2), 69–70. Available at: https://www.nepjol.info/index.php/JKMC/article/view/8140 (accessed on 17 August 2021).
24. Sim, S., (2020). Workplace sexual harassment and labor inspection: Focused on labor inspectors' experience of dealing with sexual harassment cases. Economy and Society, [Online] 128, pp. 235–265. Available at: https://www.dbpia.co.kr/journal/articleDetail?nodeId=NODE10501918&language=ko_KR (accessed on 17 August 2021).
25. Skye Schooley, (2020). Workplace Harassment: How to Recognize and Report It. [Online] Businessnewsdaily.com. Available at: https://www.businessnewsdaily.com/9426-workplace-harassment.html (accessed on 17 August 2021).
26. Subbiah, I., Markham, M., Graff, S., Matt-Amaral, L., Close, J., Griffith, K., & Jagsi, R., (2021). Sexual harassment of oncologists. Journal of Clinical Oncology, [Online] 39(15), . Available at: https://ascopubs.org/doi/10.1200/JCO.2021.39.15_suppl.11001 (accessed on 17 August 2021).

27. Subramanian, K., (2017). Sexual harassment at workplaces in Sivakasi. Journal of Politics and Governance, [Online] 6(1), 35. Available at: http://www.indianjournals.com/ijor.aspx?target=ijor:jpg&volume=6&issue=1&article=004 (accessed on 17 August 2021).
28. U.S. Department of Labor, (2012). What do I Need to Know About… Workplace Harassment. [Online] Available at: https://www.dol.gov/agencies/oasam/centers-offices/civil-rights-center/internal/policies/workplace-harassment/2012 (accessed on 17 August 2021).

Chapter 3

Sexual Harassment in Academic Sciences, Engineering, and Medicine

CONTENTS

In this chapter it suggests that academia should not be considered an exception and that it faces similar rates of sexual harassment. As much of the research on sexual harassment has focused on workplaces outside academia. To analyze the extent to which all three forms of sexual harassment occur in academia, specifically in the fields of science, engineering, and medicine and also consider the overall culture and subcultures in which it takes place, in order to identify conditions that increase the probability that sexual harassment behaviors will occur is the goal of this chapter.

Moreover, in this chapter the analysis aims to shed light on the extent to which women experience sexual harassment in science, engineering, and medicine; compare experiences across different environments; and understand how the organizational makeup of these fields contributes to the risk for sexual harassment. In addition to it, in terms of the sexual harassment this chapter reviews how academia and academic science, engineering, and medicine specifically are unique environments.

3.1. INTRODUCTION

In order to improve the recruitment, retention, and advancement of women in the fields of science, engineering, and medicine research, activity, and funding has been devoted over the last few decades. It has been seen that in recent years there is diversity in these fields and specially the participation of the women has been improved and along with this there are significantly more women entering careers and studying science, engineering, and medicine than ever before. Therefore, there are barriers and biases which are being faced by the women who enters in these fields and sexual harassment is one of the barriers which is faced by them.

In the different industries the incidence of the sexual harassment has been held steady over the 30 years, so now more women are in the workforce and in academia, and in the fields of science, engineering, and medicine (as students and faculty) and so more women are experiencing sexual harassment as they work and learn.

In the workplace revelations of the sexual harassment experienced by women over the last several years and urgent questions about the specific impact of this discriminatory behavior on women and the extent to which it is limiting their careers have been raised in the academic setting.

In the academia the sexual harassment of women explores the influence of sexual harassment on the career advancement of women in the scientific, technical, and medical workforce. The research on the extent to which women in the fields of science, engineering, and medicine are victimized by sexual harassment is being reviewed by this report and also examines the existing information on the extent to which sexual harassment in academia negatively impacts the recruitment, retention, and advancement of women pursuing scientific, engineering, technical, and medical careers.

The sexual harassment is being defined as the unwelcome sexual behavior that is offensive, humiliating or intimidating. It can be written, verbal or physical, and can happen in person or online.

It has been noted that both men and women can be the victims of sexual harassment. It may amount to sex discrimination when it happens at school, work (Figure 3.1).

- What Does it Include?

Sexual harassment can include someone:

- Touching, grabbing, or making other physical contact without consent;
- Making comments that have a sexual meaning;
- Asking for sex or sexual favors;
- Leering and staring;
- Displaying rude and offensive material so that others can see it;
- Making sexual gestures or suggestive body movements;
- Cracking sexual jokes and comments around;
- Questioning about your sex life;
- Insulting with sexual comments;
- Committing a criminal offence, such as making an obscene phone call, indecently exposing themselves or sexually assaulting.

Figure 3.1. Sexual harassment in academic sciences, engineering, and medicine.

Source: Image by Pxhere.

- When Does Sexual Harassment Become Sexual Assault?

In the case if someone is sexually harassing to another in a way that causes one to feel humiliation, pain, fear, or intimidation, then this can be considered sexual assault.

- How Sexual Harassment can Affect You?

If someone is being sexually harassed, then he or she might:

- Feel stressed, anxious, or depressed;
- Withdraw from social situations;
- Lose confidence and self-esteem;
- Have physical symptoms of stress, such as headaches, backaches, or sleep problems;
- Be less productive and unable to concentrate.
- **What Can You Do?**

It has been said that no one deserves or asks to be sexually harassed. In an environment everyone has the right to work and live, which is free from harassment, bullying, discrimination, and violence. Sexual harassment is illegal (under the Sex Discrimination Act, 1984).

Here are some things one can do:

- **Talk to the Offender:** An attempt can be made by one person to quickly resolve the situation by explaining to the person who is harassing that the behavior is unwanted.
- **Be Informed:** It has been said that if anyone is being harassed at work or school then he or she should find the policies and procedures are for preventing and handling sexual harassment.
- **Keep a Diary:** Nowadays it is necessary to make a note of everything, including when it occurred, the names of any people who saw what happened, and what can be done to stop it.
- **Save Any Evidence:** Keep text messages, social media comments, notes, and emails. This evidence can help if anyone makes a complaint.
- **Get External Information and Advice:** In every industry the rules and laws are different, so for the work situations one must check law stuff to find the union representing the industry. The options and rights of the individual's advice can be given by them. It has been said that in the case if someone does not feel comfortable pursuing the issue alone, then the other person can also act on his/her behalf. They should respect your confidentiality.
- **Tell Someone:** Sexual harassment is not something that one need to deal by themselves. In the workplace, it might be worth talking to the HR manager, who will be able to help in deciding what to do and one might also want to talk to a trusted friend or family member about what is going on.
- **Sexual Harassment Detrimentally Affects the Work Environment:** As a result of sexual and other types of harassment the affront to personal dignity that occurs, by definition, detrimentally affects the work environment. To understand the intent of a person behavior is also important, whether the behavior is face-to-face or behind another employees back which may be considered as irrelevant in determining whether or not a behavior is sexual harassment.

In the work environment the main thing is the impact of the behavior, irrespective of the intent of the behavior which may be judged on the impact on the environment. Though, the statement that the conduct was not intended to have a negative consequence is not a valid defense of harassing behavior.

A pattern of the offensive conduct is usually being required by the hostile environment and incidents of extremely offensive sexual or sex-based verbal conduct is being isolated or infrequent, particularly when perpetrated by a supervisor or coupled with physical conduct, however, may create a hostile environment.

It has been noted that the boundaries of the work environment are not determined by location. Apart from this the boundaries of the work environment are defined by whether or not the person is doing something related to his or her job.

So only for this reason in the locations which are outside the traditional work site only in that the harassment can occur. Any place where employees happen to be for work related purposes is being included by the workplace.

For a work-related activity this includes traveling to work-related conferences or branch offices, attending staff parties, attending conferences, or at the home of a colleague. The key to understanding the boundaries of the work environment is to consider whether the person is in a specific place because of their job.

Between the work environment and a situation in which colleagues or employees meet in a purely private setting, such as while attending a private party, while on vacation, or while attending a conference as a hobby a difference is being made by the U.S. and Canadian law and in the work such circumstances are not being considered.

It has been said that U.S. and Canadian law does not protect people from the harassment if the harassment occurs in these situations, unless adverse consequences are brought back to the work environment. For instance, a sexual solicitation made at a private party by a person who works for the same employer would not give rise to a complaint under the U.S. and Canadian legal systems unless the person who turned down the solicitation later suffered adverse consequences at work.

- Is Sexual Harassment about Sex or Power?

A study has been conducted by the ILO (International Labor Organization) in the year 1992 in which the sexual harassment is inextricably linked with power and takes place in societies which often treat women as sex objects and second-class citizens.

There is a writer by the name Catharine MacKinnon which is being considered one of the foremost writers on the topic, describes sexual harassment as an explosive combining of unacceptable sexual behavior and the abuse of power. It has been seen that there is always an involvement of some form of abuse of power, as a particular incident of harassment may or may not include any explicitly sexual behavior.

For instance, at the woman work when a harasser makes interruptions, then it means he is not engaging in any kind of romantic sexual action and at that time he is engaged in aggression. This situation is quite similar to that of the street harasser who comments on a woman body, as she walks by the co-worker who won't stop touching her or the landlord and who won't repair the sink because she was not nice to him. So, these all are the forms of the sexual harassment.

To closely examine the sexual aspect of the sexual harassment it is very important because sexuality is often used as a justification for this social practice and there is a confusion about the difference between sexual invitation and sexual harassment is common.

It has been seen that there are many individuals around the world who all are having a similar thought process about the sexual harassment, as they all believe that sexual harassment is a practice based on simple sexual attraction. For the women it is often seen as an expression of male interest and a form of flattering sexual attention and a sometimes vulgar but essentially harmless romantic game, well within the range of normal, acceptable behavior between men and women.

Therefore, with the use of the power the difference between invitation and harassment can be understood. Harassment is not a method of courtship and it is not meant to appeal to women. It has been said that it can only put pressure on the women and not attract them. In the encounter when the recipient of sexual harassment has no choice or has reason to fear the repercussions if she declines, the interaction has moved out of the realm of invitation and courtship into the arena of intimidation and aggression. From reacting to harassers with strong, effective countermeasures the confusions about the dynamics of sexuality and power in sexual harassment prevents women.

3.2. TYPES OF SEXUAL HARASSMENT

3.2.1. Gender Harassment

It is considered as the generalized sexist statements and behavior that convey insulting or degrading attitudes about women or men. Examples: insulting remarks, obscene jokes, or humor about sex, etc.

3.2.2. Seductive Behavior

It has been considered as the unwanted, inappropriate, and offensive sexual advances. There are some of the examples which include repeated and unwanted sexual invitation; insistent requests for dates/dinner/drinks; persistent letters, phone calls, etc.

3.2.3. Sexual Bribery

Solicitation of sexual activity or other sex-linked behavior by promise of reward; the proposition may be either overt or subtle.

3.2.4. Sexual Coercion

Coercion of sexual activity or other sex-linked behavior by threat of punishment; examples include negative performance evaluations, withholding of promotion, threat of termination.

3.2.5. Sexual Imposition

Gross sexual imposition (such as forceful touching, feeling, grabbing), or sexual assault/battery (Figure 3.2).

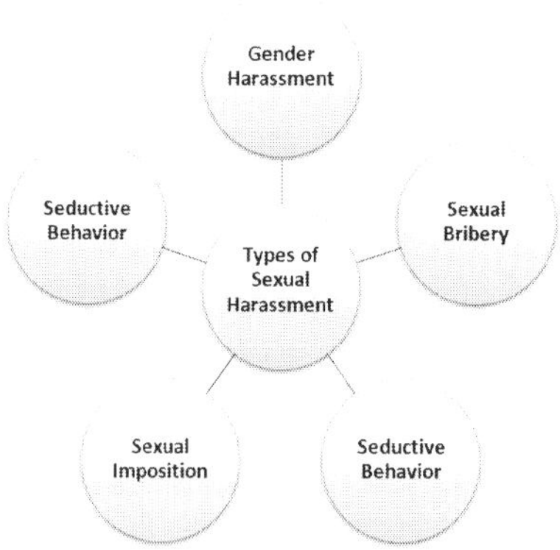

Figure 3.2. Types of sexual harassment.

3.3. REACTIONS/EFFECTS

It has been said that being sexually harassed can impact psychological health, physical well-being, and vocational development. Psychological and physical reactions to being harassed may include the following subsections.

3.3.1. Physiological Reactions

- Headaches;
- Gastrointestinal distress;
- Sleep disturbances, nightmares;
- Lethargy;
- Dermatological reactions;
- Weight fluctuation;
- Sexual problems;
- Phobias, panic reactions.

3.3.2. Psychological Reactions

- Depression, anxiety, shock, denial;
- Confusion, feelings of being powerless;
- Anger, fear, frustration, irritability;
- Shame, self-consciousness, low self-esteem;
- Insecurity, embarrassment, feelings of betrayal;
- Guilt, self-blame, isolation.

3.3.3. Career-Related Effects

- Decreased job satisfaction;
- Absenteeism;
- Unfavorable performance evaluations;
- Withdrawal from work or school;
- Loss of job or promotion;
- Change in career goals, jobs, educational programs, academic majors, etc.;
- Drop in academic/work performance due to stress (Figure 3.3).

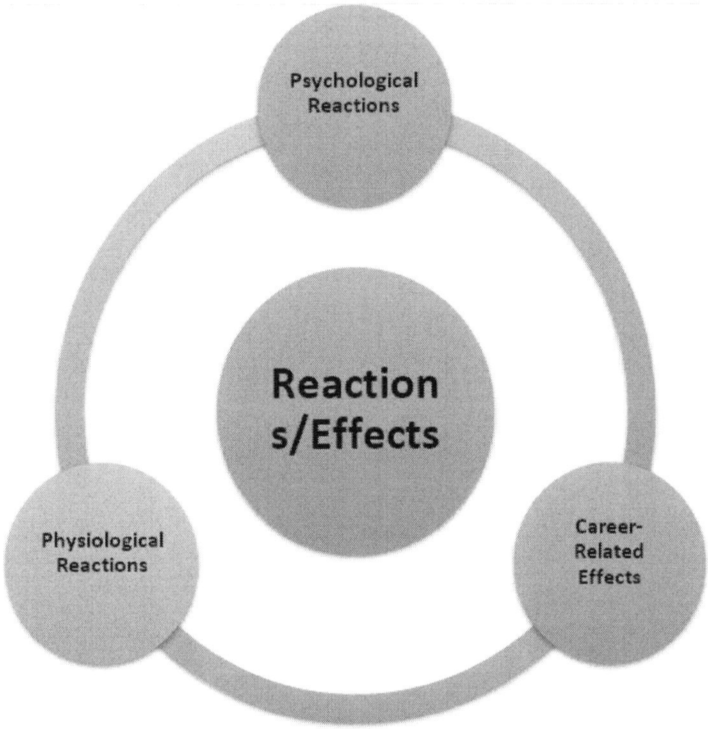

Figure 3.3. Reactions or effects of sexual harassment.

3.4. THE ACADEMIC ENVIRONMENT IN SCIENCE, ENGINEERING, AND MEDICINE

Against the women there are some of the main conditions that increase the risk of sexual harassment being perpetrated, which are organizational tolerance for sexual harassment and male-dominated environments are the one which gets appear in the academia generally, and specifically within the fields of science, engineering, and medicine.

As the permissive environments the higher education environments are being perceived in part because when targets report, they are either retaliated against or nothing happens to the perpetrator. It has been seen that in the recent paper there is one respondent who reported her experience of psychological and physical harassment from her advisor described the response to her reporting the experience in this way. So, in this case it has been seen that the only choice which has been given is to leave the department even after talking to the faculty director or the chair of the department. It has been noted that after leaving the institution next year this advisor got three more students.

With these types of cases higher education is also full where the offenders are an open secret but are not sanctioned. Some of the issues are being reviled in the interview which was conducted by RTI International with female faculty in science, engineering, and medicine who experienced sexually harassing behavior and that also explain this general climate of accepting sexual harassment.

The behavior of the mail colleagues is being demonstrated in the interview response and the male who are at higher ranking faculty or administrators perceived as "superstars" in their particular substantive area, was often minimized or ignored. Even though men who did not have the superstar label were often described as receiving preferential treatment and excused for gender-biased and sexually harassing behavior.

There is a thought by some people that people are blinded by good signs and shiny personalities. This is because those things tend to go hand in hand. As nobody wants to think about the person who is doing incredible work in getting all these grants and someone who has created a negative environment for others. This thing has been experienced by many people again and again.

In the interview data there is a theme that emerged was that respondents and other colleagues often clearly knew which individuals had a history of sexually harassing behavior. By both male and female colleagues, the warning is being provided and to take actions against these perpetrators was fruitless which was often accompanied by advice that trying and that the best options for dealing with the behavior were to avoid or ignore it (Figure 3.4).

Among the women faculty there are many respondents who described the dialog in order to warn about or disclose sexually harassing behaviors as an unfortunate shared bond that was far too often the norm.

As an excuse, expectations around behavior were often noted for older generations of faculty, primarily men, to perpetrate sexually harassing behavior. Within the academic settings there are many respondents who noted that the "old guard," in perpetrating this type of behavior, was doing what they have always done and was not likely to change, because of a general acceptance.

Figure 3.4. The academic environment in science, engineering, and medicine.

Source: Image by the Blue Diamond Gallery.

It is a kind of new thing and the mindset is so ingrained, like the people say these things and they also do not even realize their intent, which is not to sexually harass the people, but they do it automatically, and they do not even think about it.

As fueling this behavior, the normalization of sexual harassment and gender bias was also noted in new cohorts of sciences, engineering, and medicine faculty. With the unbiased views and the respectful behavior respondents discussed the disheartening experiences of colleagues who entered training settings, but who concluded those experiences endorsing or dismissing sexually harassing and gender-biased behavior among themselves and others.

No one thinks that the prospect of being sexually assaulted was as bad as watching the next generation of sexual harassers being formed. It is considered to be the worst part.

Across the multiple institutions sometimes it takes many reports for a preparator's actions which is to even to be acknowledged. This reality, as well as the perception widely held across higher education, means that few targets believe their complaints will be taken seriously. As there are many American colleges and the universities which were formed for the express purpose to educate men, higher education environments are also often historically male dominated, and science, engineering, and medicine in higher education are still numerically and culturally male dominated.

Since 2000 women have earned more than half of all science and engineering bachelor's degrees and due to the high concentration of women in only a handful of specific scientific fields academic science and engineering as a whole continues to be very male dominated.

It has been said that men and women tend to fall into different fields of study as the National Science Foundation's 2016 Science and Engineering Indicators points out and at all levels of higher education degree attainment these tendencies are consistent.

In engineering men earned 80.7% of bachelor's degrees which are being awarded, 82% in computer sciences, and 80.9% in physics in the year 2013. On the other hand, women earned half or more of the bachelor's degrees in psychology, biological sciences, agricultural sciences, and all the broad fields within social sciences except for economics.

It has been noted that they are vastly underrepresented at the faculty level even in biology-related fields where women make up more than one-half of all doctorate recipients. There is study which is being conducted by the Jason and Joan (2014) in which they published the Proceedings of the National Academy of Sciences found that of 2,062 life sciences faculty members at top-ranked programs in the United States (U.S.), only 21% of full professors and 29% of assistant professors were women.

For several decades women have been earning medical degrees in numbers at least equal to men in medicine and the female medical school faculty neither advance as rapidly nor are compensated as well as their male colleagues.

In the career advancement a survey was conducted by the Association of American Medical Colleges further reveal the disparities between men and women: 1 in 6 department chairs or deans were women in 2013–2014, up from 1 in 10 in 2003–2004; 38%, only a little more than a third, of full-time academic medicine faculty are women; and only 21% of full professors are women, as are 34% of full-time associate professors.

It has been said that where boundaries between work and personal life are blurred and one is always working are particularly difficult on people with child care or elder care responsibilities is the culture of higher education workplaces and as well as for the people as well as for people who do not conform to gendered expectations for behavior or appearance. These people are most often considered as the women and sexual- and gender-minority people. In history, it has been seen that the life of the mind was believed to be men's work, and while the society may have more enlightened views today on the contributions of women to higher education generally and science specifically, the structure of the academic workplace is still one best suited to men who have a wife at home serving as domestic caretaker full time. In academia this is the ideal work norm which is pervasive. On a broader conceptualization of gender harassment Leskinen and Cortina explain this thing in their work.

A person who is dedicated towards the work full time consistently during his or her lifetime and who also does not take leaves for pregnancy, child care, or other care-giving responsibilities is considered to be the ideal worker. Apart from the inherent stereotypical sex-based expectations (i.e., workplaces are structured around male bodies) that this ideal endorses, the employees' value and reward the ideal worker.

There are some of the employers who punish the workers, if they get fail to meet the ideal worker norm, as this notion of "family responsibilities discrimination" is gaining attention among lawyers and social scientists as a significant barrier to women's employment and advancement.

In addition to it, academic science, engineering, and medicine are hierarchical. On the principal investigators students have to rely on at the graduate level who control funding, research direction, and recruitment decisions.

The training encourages a respect and trust of those at the top of the hierarchy in academic medicine, as there are clear hierarchical roles which are started with attending physicians, followed by fellows, residents, and interns, and then medical students at the bottom. Due to experience or expertise hierarchy operates out of habit rather than as something that is constantly reflected on and justified and also the misuse of power can increase.

In science, engineering, and medicine the nature of mentoring creates unique risks for trainees. In the lab or in the field or in the hospital and sometimes in isolated environments the mentor-mentee relationship can involve much time spent alone together.

On one mentor it also involves the significant dependence or a small committee because research projects, education, and career mentoring, and funding are often all tied to the advisor and not in the control of the student.

In the hospital settings training specifically takes place in the medical field over 24-hour call periods. Under the direction of faculty attending physicians who may or may not be physically present in the hospital for the educational benefits, the interns, and residents (even the nomenclature attests to the trainees having a special relationship to the hospital training space) provide much of the patient care.

Especially in the emergency room, the operating rooms, and the intensive care units is obviously very intense, tiring, and stressful, interns caring for the sick patients and also because of the requirement for extended duty hours, call rooms with single or multiple beds are close by for when sleep is possible. For the sexual harassment and sexual assault, the risk they pose should be obvious.

In addition to it, in all levels of the medical hierarchy research on the medical environment reveals that overall "mistreatment" is commonplace, especially among medical school students, interns, and residents in all specialties.

In environments with little structure or accountability for the faculty member, and a decreased ability for students to leave without professional repercussions these environmental and mentoring factors mean that there are increased opportunities for sexual harassment perpetration.

It has been noted that substantial gender disparities exist within academic science, engineering, and medicine. From the frequency these range with which the men invite women to speak at conferences, in order to know how competent and employable female students are perceived, the degree to which women and men self-cite and the extent to which women feel they can make use of family-friendly policies even when they exist.

Over research-intensive one's women are also more likely to hold teaching-intensive faculty positions and for the number of women in science the national numbers appear to be increasing and they are clustered in institutions where graduate students are not being trained, federal funding is less frequent, and in general are places where faculty receive less support to conduct independent work and contribute to the process of science.

In recent years the number of women appears to be increasing in the sciences and the reality is that only white women are increasing in numbers, and women of color are on the decline. This is not considered as the mission of this report and a note should be made that the gender discrimination itself harms women and the broader meritocracy of science.

Therefore, it concludes that the for the sexual harassment gender discrimination and male domination are features of the academic science, engineering, and medicine climate that create a permissive environment.

3.5. SEXUAL HARASSMENT OF FACULTY AND STAFF

On the sexual harassment prevalence, the best meta-analysis to the date has been done. It has been seen that 58% of female academic faculty and staff experienced sexual harassment, as this is being reviled by the Ilies and colleagues.

Furthermore, sexual harassment in the private sector government, and military samples is being examined by the meta-analysis to the academic setting. The survey found that the academic workplace had the second highest rate, behind the military (69%) and this has been found only when comparing the academic workplace with the other workplaces.

On par the government and the private sector sample with each other with 43% and 46%, respectively. It has been said that all the top workplaces are both males dominated than the private sector and the government, demonstrating the significance this has on rates of harassment, and also suggesting that in areas of academia that are more male dominated and the rates of sexually harassing behavior may be higher.

In academia more recent study has been done analyzing the experiences of women and men working and the court system and military, the connection to male-dominated workplaces was confirmed for academia. At a unit level it has been demonstrated that when the underrepresentation of women increased one unit, the odds that women would face gender harassment (a type of sexual harassment) increased 1.2 times.

From the other workplaces research has also confirmed the general finding for the female faculty and staff in academia that the majority of the sexual harassment experienced was gender harassment and that the other two types of sexual harassment were rarely experienced without gender harassment also occurring. This pattern has been documented and the gender harassment being far more prevalent that other types of sexual harassment persist today.

As the university employees the students perform the function and their focus is the experiences of graduate students. As per their research, the majority of harassment experiences involved sexist or sexually offensive language, gestures, or pictures (59.1%), with 6.4% involving unwanted sexual attention, 4.7% involving unwanted touching, and 3.5% involving subtle or explicit bribes or threats.

It should also be noted that sexual harassment can be bottom-up, coming from those who have less formal power in the organization, and the researchers often refer to this as contra power harassment. For example, in academia O'Connell and Korabik reported that 42% of their sample of women were working, as they had encountered sexually harassing conduct from men at lower levels in the organizational hierarchy.

Many other studies have been resounding, that some of this subordinate-perpetrated harassment was gender harassment (e.g., insulting remarks about women, vulgar gestures, lewd jokes). It has been reported that at a large research university 48% of women faculty had encountered sexually harassing conduct from students; most commonly, this behavior entailed sexist comments (defined as "jokes or remarks that are stereotypical or derogatory to members of your sex").

As the perpetrators virtually all instances involved men. To rape the student-on-faculty sexual harassment escalated in one of the cases. It has been noted that even in situations in which a woman has clearly defined authority to explain the dynamics underlying contra power harassment and the gender continues to be one of the most salient and powerful variables governing work relations.

There is an argument which is being made that the gender-based norms seep into the workplace as per the concept of sex-role spillover. The lower status of the women is being reflected by the contra power sexual harassment in the society which is relative to the men and it also replicates the hierarchy in the organization. In addition to it, students have a certain degree of power over faculty when student evaluations influence promotion or reward decisions in the academic context.

The science, engineering, and medicine committee contracted RTI International to gather a clearer picture of what the sexually harassing experiences were of women faculty and also to conduct a series of interviews with women who had experienced at least one sexually harassing behavior in the past 5 years.

Their responses have been varied at the time when these women were asked to describe the most impactful experience and also included sexual advances, lewd jokes or comments, disparaging or critical comments related to competency, unwanted sexual touching, stalking, and sexual assault by a colleague (Figure 3.5).

Figure 3.5. Sexual harassment of faculty and staff.

Source: Image by Picpedia.org.

In the terms of unwanted sexual advances there is one respondent who observed that most persons understood sexual harassment primarily, but that gender-based harassment in academic settings was both widespread and impactful.

In the workplace there is the demand of many to shut the mouth of the woman and demeaning her in front of other colleagues, telling her that she is not as capable as others are, or telling others that she is not [as] sincere as people are. Mind games have been played so that women cannot perform physically, so it is more of intellectual level stress.

As the sexual harassment most of the respondents characterized their experiences at the time of interview. Therefore, there are some of the respondents who noted that they had not immediately recognized those experiences as such.

By the pervasive acceptance of gender-discriminatory behavior delayed awareness of sexual harassment was heavily influenced within the academic context. Within their departments there are many respondents who reported that they were the only woman or one of a few women.

In the male-dominated gender discrimination was often normalized settings in which they worked, which interviewees believed had fueled sexually harassing behavior, fostered tolerance of it, and made differentiating it as such difficult.

3.6. SEXUAL HARASSMENT OF TRAINEES

For the undergraduate student's effort to develop a campus climate survey that could be used across institutions, researchers at RTI International conducted a nine-school pilot campus climate survey. On the sexual assault primarily, the researchers focused and on harassment the survey questions were limited to crude sexual behavior and some forms of unwanted sexual attention.

In the academic year 2014–2015 there was a survey which determined that the prevalence of female undergraduates who experienced crude behavior and no assault forms of unwanted sexual attention also ranged from 14% to as high as 46% in some universities.

In order to identify who, the perpetrators were the survey module did not include questions that would allow researchers and therefore it is not clear whether the perpetrators were students, university staff, or faculty.

In October 2014, Georgia State University a second effort has been started convened a forum on campus sexual assault and harassment, which led to the development of the Administrator-Researcher Campus Climate Collaborative, referred to as ARC3, and which is led by Sarah L.

With guidance from leading sexual violence researchers a comprehensive survey instrument of sexual misconduct was developed and the student affairs, Title IX professionals, campus law enforcement, target/victim advocates, and counselors. About the status of the perpetrator the survey was developed for undergraduate and graduate students and included questions.

On the sexual experiences questionnaire (SEQ) the ARC3 used state-of-the-art instruments based to ask behavior-based questions measuring sexual harassment, including all of its subtypes: gender harassment (broken down into sexist hostility and crude behavior), unwanted sexual attention, and sexual coercion.

To measure their campus climate 150 institutions of higher education have used the ARC3 survey till the date. In their system multiple campuses across their institution have been evaluated by two of those institutions Penn State University and the University of Texas System and therefore included a large sample across multiple fields.

The most common form of the sexual harassment is the gender harassment as per the result and that women are sexually harassed more often than men. For students the overall rates of the sexual harassment at these two institutions which are ranged between 20 and 50% depending on what level of education (undergraduate or graduate) they were in and what the student major was.

It has been noted that to experience the sexual harassment by faculty and staff, female medical students were 220% more likely than non-SEM majors and on the other hand female engineering students were 34% more likely than non-SEM majors to experience it.

In one type of the sexual harassment the student experienced the crude harassment and interestingly there was a significant difference in it. By faculty or staff, to experience crude harassment female medical students were 149% more likely than not in science, engineering, and medicine (non-SEM) majors while female engineering students experienced it at the same level as non-SEM and science students experienced it (8–9%, compared to 18% for female medical students).

It has been seen that in the medical school or in a college of medicine student reported having experienced some form of sexual harassment.

There has been conducted and by using the ARC3 survey it has been found that 525 graduate students regarding their exposure to sexual harassment and found that more than one-third (38%) of female graduate students experienced sexual harassment from faculty or staff, compared with only 23.4% of male graduate students (Figure 3.6).

Figure 3.6. Sexual harassment of trainees.

Source: Image by Max Pixel.

As per the study it has been seen that in the higher education institutions the sexual harassment is common and that the female graduate students face higher rates of sexual harassment from faculty and staff compared with their male counterparts.

By the students-on-students sexual harassment can also be perpetrated. As per the online survey the Association of American University Women 2005 used a non-SEQ set of behavior-based questions that left out sexist comments and focused on sexual behavior, found that 62% of all undergraduates had experienced sexual harassment.

It has been seen those questions about the perpetrated is being included in the research and also the results showed that at college-related events and activities, peer harassment was significantly more common than harassment and by the faculty 80% of students who were harassed reported it was from peers or former peers and only 18% reported it was from faculty or staff.

As it has been noted that peer harassment is being measured by the ARC3 survey and it has also been noted that ARC3 survey does not focus on any particular location when measuring experiences of sexual harassment. In any number of the environments the respondents can report on the student for conducting the occurring and the both educational (e.g., classrooms, lectures, laboratories, libraries, patient rooms, surgical suites) and social (parties, bars, gyms, cafes, concerts, apartments, etc.).

To make the difference between the harassing conduct a major caveat of this measure is that it is not sensitive enough from non-harassing, social-sexual behaviors from other students (e.g., sexual joking, flirting among friends).

For instance, if the complaint is being made by the female student that a fellow student distributed sexually suggestive materials or repeatedly asked her out on dates, there is no way to know whether this was upsetting versus humorous versus innocuous to her and because of this blending of potentially offensive and inoffensive conduct, the result may be inflated prevalence estimates of student-on-student sexual harassment.

3.7. SEXUAL HARASSMENT WITHIN THE SCIENCES

In the sciences the following section describes studies that have been examined the sexual harassment and the experiences of the women. In the year 2015 a study has been conducted in which it has been shown that 474 astronomers and planetary scientists found that women who experienced sexist comments were much more likely to be trainees (students) at the time and slightly more likely to experience it from peers or others at the same rank or level in the formal institutional hierarchy than from superiors.

According to the studies, the women are more likely than the men to report experiencing sexual harassment which is being supported by the other findings.

About the other forms of harassment, the study also asked the respondents including the racial harassment and also asked whether they felt unsafe in their position because of either their gender or race. To report feeling unsafe the study found that women were more likely than men because of their gender (30% of women respondents versus 2% of men respondents) and that respondents of color were more likely to report feeling unsafe because of their race (24% versus 1% of white respondents).

To experience the verbal racial harassment women of color were the most likely and that to experience verbal sexual harassment they were equally likely as white women. In addition to it, to report feeling unsafe compared with men of color, white women, or white men, and almost 1 in 2 women of color reported feeling unsafe women of color were most likely because of their gender (40% based on gender and 28% based on race).

Other research on women of color is being supported by this study and that shows women of color experience more harassment (as a combination of sexual and racial harassment) and thus are likely to be having more negative experiences than other groups.

In total, with similar environmental variables planetary science fields are experiencing sexual harassment at a level similar to other workplaces and this research adds to the growing evidence that white women and women of color in the astronomy.

It has been said that the part of the scientific scholarship is an important part of the field research and but it is also an environment that can present increased risks for sexual harassment. To a hostile environment a survey of academic field experiences (the SAFE study) identified systemic and problematic behaviors in scientific field sites that may lead.

Several characteristics of field-site environments is being identified by the study and the sexual harassment that occurs: with few respondents being aware of available reporting mechanisms there was a lack of awareness regarding codes of conduct and sexual harassment policies and the targets of sexually harassing behavior in field sites were primarily women trainees and perpetrators varied between men and women when women were harassed, perpetrators were primarily senior to the trainees; however, when men were harassed, it was typically by a peer.

To reach this diverse population of field scientist Clancy and the colleagues used a snowball sampling technique and of those that responded, 64% (both men and women) had personally experienced sexual harassment in field sites in the form of inappropriate sexual remarks, comments about physical appearances or cognitive sex differences, or sexist or demeaning jokes, and more than 20% of respondents reported having personally experienced sexual assault (Figure 3.7).

Figure 3.7. Sexual harassment within the sciences.

Source: Image by Piqsels logo.

At the field sites the research also found that harassment and assault were primarily targeted at trainees (students and postdocs), and specifically that 90% of the women who were harassed were trainees or employees when they were targeted at the field site. In the field sites the research found that women primarily experienced sexual harassment that came from someone superior to them in the field-site hierarchy significantly. By the superiors this higher likelihood of the harassment being perpetrated and it is being perhaps as the unique characteristics that distinguishes research field sites from other workplace settings where it is more common for the harassment to come from peers.

In understanding the severity of the sexual harassment experienced this characteristic of field sites is important because the outcomes from sexual harassment can be worse if it comes from a superior who has power over the target.

A thematic analysis of 26 interviews of women and men field scientists is being performed by the SAFE team in a 2017 follow-up. It has been seen that the first finding of this chapter was that respondents had very different experiences of field sites where rules were absent, where they were present, and where they were present and enforced and were ones where the respondents described sexual harassment and assault experiences.

After this there is the second finding which says that the scientists who were sexually harassed or experienced other incivilities had worse career experiences, also matches the broader workplace aggression literature.

In the end the authors found that egalitarian field sites were ones that set a positive example for scientists, had fewer incivilities, sexual harassment experiences, and sexual assault, and created positive experiences for respondents that reaffirmed their commitment to science.

These data point a way forward, for sexual harassment in science work and education settings are similar to those of other workplaces in the sense that organizational antecedents, and that therefore for reducing sexual harassment in science the literature provides strong, evidence-based recommendations.

3.8. SEXUAL HARASSMENT WITHIN MEDICINE

By the RTI International the interviews are being conducted. Those unique settings such as medical residencies were described as breeding grounds for abusive behavior by superiors. At this stage of medical career respondents expressed that this was largely and the expectation of this behavior was widely accepted.

In training setting the expectations of the abusive, grueling conditions caused the several respondents to view sexual harassment as a part of the continuum of what they were expected to endure. As it has been noted that one respondent is about residency training if everyone is having human rights violations. So, it is just like the tolerable sexual harassment.

From the campuses with the exception of the ARC3 data with medical schools, unfortunately, much of the survey research conducted on the medical fields has not followed good practices for surveys on sexual harassment. From these surveys the prevalence numbers on the medical field are not comparable and may be underreporting the rate of sexual harassment in these fields.

There is one significant problem which is attached with comparing much of the data on the medical fields with other workplaces is the consistency of definitions used. From the result of the sexual harassment verbal harassment is being separated and while they include verbal harassment in the form of sexist jokes as sexual harassment, they omit verbal harassment such as being called derogatory name.

There are some of the other instances while some items combine and mix measures of sexual harassment with gender discrimination and the survey item that asks whether sexual harassment is occurring omits the crude behavior part of gender harassment which will result in measurement of a much broader set of experiences.

In the medicine it has been seen that the research can identify some characteristics of how sexual harassment occurs. In the medicine research that has examined different specialties, female surgeons and physicians in specialties that are historically male dominated are more likely to be harassed than those in other specialties, but only when they are in training.

At the same rates once they are out of their residency and in practice, they experience harassment as the other specialties. In surgery these researchers suggested that for women in surgery and the emergency medicine the higher rates of sexual harassment might be due to those fields having and valuing a hierarchical and authoritative workplace.

Especially among the leaders, the preponderance of men in surgery and emergency medicine is also likely a large factor in explaining the high harassment in these fields. In the two other studies it has been seen that students perceived the experiences to be more common in the general surgery specialty than in others and in specialty other research reveals that respondents reported their perceptions of these harassing environments influenced their choice (Figure 3.8).

Figure 3.8. Sexual harassment within medicine.

Source: Image by Max Pixel.

On the medical setting other research suggests that sexual harassment may be worse depending, for instance, women perceived sexual harassment and gender discrimination to be more common in academic medical centers than in community hospitals and outpatient office settings.

The one important finding from the research on the environment of academic medical centers is that in addition to students, trainees, and faculty being harassed by colleagues and those in leadership, they are also reporting harassment perpetrated by patients and patients' families. From patients and the patients' families it is very common and is one of the top sources of the harassment they experience.

3.9. CONCLUSION

Overall, it has been seen that at least there are four characteristics which are being exhibited that create higher level of risk for the sexual harassment to occur that is male dominated environment, organizational tolerance for sexually harassing behavior, hierarchical, and dependent relationships between faculty and their trainees and the isolated environments.

It has been noted that in academic science, medicine, and engineering the sexual harassment is common and greater than 50% of women faculty and staff and 20–50% of women students encounter or experience sexually harassing conduct in academia.

REFERENCES

1. (2010). Sexual Harassment. [eBook] Center for Victim Advocacy and Violence Prevention. Available at: https://www.usf.edu/student-affairs/victim-advocacy/types-of-crimes/sexualharassment.pdf (accessed on 17 August 2021).
2. (2018). Sexual Harassment of Women. [Online] Available at: https://www.nap.edu/read/24994/chapter/1#iii (accessed on 17 August 2021).
3. Andrea, W., & Linda, W., (2021). Sexual harassment and its aftershocks. C&EN Global Enterprise, [Online] 99(9), pp. 28–35. Available at: https://pubs.acs.org/doi/abs/10.1021/cen-09909-cover (accessed on 17 August 2021).
4. Benya, F., Widnall, S., & Johnson, P., (2018). Sexual Harassment in Academic Sciences, Engineering, and Medicine. [Online] Ncbi.nlm.nih.gov. Available at: https://www.ncbi.nlm.nih.gov/books/NBK519457/ (accessed on 17 August 2021).
5. Boyd, C., (2010). The debate over the prohibition of romance in the workplace. Journal of Business Ethics, [Online] 97(2), 325–338. Available at: https://link.springer.com/article/10.1007%2Fs10551-010-0512-3 (accessed on 17 August 2021).
6. Carter, C. S., (2015). Sexual harassment. The Encyclopedia of Crime and Punishment, [Online] pp. 1–4. Available at: https://onlinelibrary.wiley.com/doi/10.1002/9781118519639.wbecpx138 (accessed on 17 August 2021).
7. Dougherty, D., & Meyer, M., (2015). Sexual harassment. The International Encyclopedia of Interpersonal Communication, [Online] pp. 1–8. Available at: https://onlinelibrary.wiley.com/doi/10.1002/9781118540190.wbeic260 (accessed on 17 August 2021).
8. Enyedi, L., & Cabrera, M., (2021). Sexual harassment in ophthalmology. Women in Ophthalmology, [Online] pp. 139–147. Available at: https://link.springer.com/chapter/10.1007%2F978-3-030-59335-3_19 (accessed on 17 August 2021).
9. Fiedler, A., & Hamby, E., (2000). Sexual harassment in the workplace. JONA: The Journal of Nursing Administration, [Online] 30(10), pp. 497–503. Available at: https://journals.lww.com/jonajournal/Abstract/2000/10000/Sexual_Harassment_in_the_Workplace__Nurses_.8.aspx (accessed on 17 August 2021).

10. Glicken, M., & Robinson, B., (2013). Sexual harassment in the workplace. Treating Worker Dissatisfaction During Economic Change, [Online] pp. 59–79. Available at: https://www.sciencedirect.com/science/article/pii/B978012397006000004X?via%3Dihub (accessed on 17 August 2021).
11. Hersch, J., (2015). Sexual harassment in the workplace. IZA World of Labor, [Online] Available at: https://wol.iza.org/articles/sexual-harassment-in-workplace (accessed on 17 August 2021).
12. Hersch, J., (2018). Valuing the risk of workplace sexual harassment. Journal of Risk and Uncertainty, [Online] 57(2), 111–131. Available at: https://link.springer.com/article/10.1007/s11166-018-9288-0 (accessed on 17 August 2021).
13. HR Library, (2003). Sexual Harassment-What is Sexual Harassment? [Online] Hrlibrary.umn.edu. Available at: http://hrlibrary.umn.edu/svaw/harassment/explore/1whatis.htm#harasser (accessed on 17 August 2021).
14. Kim, S., & Kleiner, B., (1999). Sexual harassment in the workplace. Equal Opportunities International, [Online] 18(2/3/4), pp. 20–22. Available at: https://www.emerald.com/insight/content/doi/10.1108/02610159910785745/full/html (accessed on 17 August 2021).
15. Michelle, J., (2014). Sexual Harassment and Sexual Bullying (for Teens)-Nemours Kidshealth. [Online] Kidshealth.org. Available at: https://kidshealth.org/en/teens/harassment.html (accessed on 17 August 2021).
16. Newman, C., & Templeton, K., (2021). Sexual harassment. A Scientific Framework for Compassion and Social Justice, [Online] pp. 252–260. Available at: https://www.taylorfrancis.com/chapters/edit/10.4324/9781003132011-39/sexual-harassment-connie-newman-kim-templeton (accessed on 17 August 2021).
17. Newman, M., Jackson, R., & Baker, D., (2003). Sexual harassment in the federal workplace. Public Administration Review, [Online] 63(4), pp. 472–483. Available at: https://onlinelibrary.wiley.com/doi/10.1111/1540-6210.00309 (accessed on 17 August 2021).
18. Ondeck, D., (1999). Sexual harassment in the workplace. Home Health Care Management and Practice, [Online] 12(1), pp. 54, 55. Available at: https://journals.sagepub.com/doi/10.1177/108482239901200114 (accessed on 17 August 2021).

19. Raihan, T., Islam, T., & Uddin, M., (2020). Sexual harassment at workplace: A systematic review of literature. Business Perspective Review, [Online] 2(2), pp. 1–14. Available at: https://riiopenjournals.com/index.php/business-perspective-review/article/view/128 (accessed on 17 August 2021).
20. Ramanathan, M., Sukanya, R., & Sarma, S., (2004). Survey on sexual harassment in the workplace. Indian Journal of Medical Ethics, [Online] 2. Available at: http://ijme.in/articles/survey-on-sexual-harassment-in-the-workplace/?galley=html (accessed on 17 August 2021).
21. Reach Out, (2021). What is Sexual Harassment? [Online] Au.reachout.com. Available at: https://au.reachout.com/articles/what-is-sexual-harassment (accessed on 17 August 2021).
22. Sheffey, S., & Tindale, R., (1992). Perceptions of sexual harassment in the workplace. Journal of Applied Social Psychology, [Online] 22(19), pp. 1502–1520. Available at: https://onlinelibrary.wiley.com/doi/10.1111/j.1559-1816.1992.tb00963.x (accessed on 17 August 2021).
23. Valente, S., & Bullough, V., (2004). Sexual harassment of nurses in the workplace. Journal of Nursing Care Quality, [Online] 19(3), 234–241. Available at: https://journals.lww.com/jncqjournal/Abstract/2004/07000/Sexual_Harassment_of_Nurses_in_the_Workplace.10.aspx (accessed on 17 August 2021).
24. Zook, R., (2000). Sexual harassment in the workplace. American Journal of Nursing, [Online] 100(12), p. 24AAAA. Available at: https://journals.lww.com/ajnonline/Abstract/2000/12000/Sexual_Harassment_in_the_Workplace.33.aspx; https://www.jstor.org/stable/3522184?origin=crossref (accessed on 17 August 2021).
25. Zuffoletto, J., (1992). Sexual harassment in the workplace. AORN Journal, [Online] 55(2), 614–616. Available at: https://aornjournal.onlinelibrary.wiley.com/doi/abs/10.1016/S0001-2092%2807%2968626-8 (accessed on 17 August 2021).

Chapter 4

Organizational Responsibility to Prevent, Prohibit, and Redress Sexual Harassment at the Workplace

CONTENTS

This chapter sheds light on the organizational responsibility in order to prevent, prohibit, and redress sexual harassment at the workplace. It begins with preventing the sexual harassment, different policies implemented in this regard. In the prevention of the sexual harassment, there are different aspects which is discussed such as the employer responsibilities and employee responsibility.

It addresses the duties of employer under prevention of sexual harassment (POSH) act, the instruments to check this issue. It also outlines the different steps in order to stop sexual harassment at the workplace that is through adopting the different policies and scopes, establishing complaints channels, etc.

In the end, it highlights the preventing the and responding factors to sexual harassment, which includes employers and housing providers.

4.1. INTRODUCTION

It has to be ensured that world of work is free from the discrimination and the violence which is considered as core for the realizing the decent work. As central to any of the system of human rights protection the principles of non-discrimination and equality are recognized internationally and in most countries' constitutions it has been embedded and also in the human rights treaties.

It has been noted that for the social justice and sustainable development there is non-discrimination and equal opportunity and treatment are considered to be basic human and labor rights in the world of work.

There is declaration which is made by the ILO by the name Declaration of Philadelphia of 1944, which says that all human beings, irrespective of race, creed, or sex, have the right to pursue both their material well-being and their spiritual development in conditions of freedom and dignity, of economic security and equal opportunity, and that discrimination constitutes a violation of rights enunciated by the Universal Declaration of Human Rights (UDHR).

In the year 1958 states adopted the Discrimination (Employment and Occupation) Convention after the adoption of the ILO Declaration of Philadelphia which has taken about 15 years. At work to protect all person against the discrimination is the aim of this convention and it also requires approving of state in order to make sure that there is protection against discrimination in employment and occupation on seven grounds, namely race, color, sex, religion, political opinion, national extraction, and social origin, as well as other grounds prohibited in national legislation by governments after consultation with the representative employers' and workers' organizations.

There are some of the states which makes sure that Convention No. 111 belongs to the fundamental ILO Conventions and it is considered as the most comprehensive international instrument which is more dedicated to guide national legislation on the promotion of non-discrimination and equality in the world of work.

It has been seen that in the workplaces the principles of non-discrimination and equality are widely accepted and the Convention has been ratified by 172 member States including India and thus to uphold the human rights of workers there is a need to express their commitments and also progressively incorporate equality and non-discrimination principles in the world of work and other laws and regulations.

It has been noted that there are various forms of discrimination continue to prevail in the world of work preventing women and men to enjoy decent work, in order to eliminate discrimination and to promote equality of opportunity and treatment, apart from the international consensus and the commitment at the national level.

Within the requirement of the Convention there is one form of discrimination on the ground of sex that should be addressed is the sexual harassment.

Against the both men and women the sexual harassment can be perpetuated. Therefore, in the workplace the majority of cases of sexual harassment are perpetuated by men against women as women often do not have equal status as men, lack power, and are in more vulnerable and insecure positions.

It has been said that due to the varying definitions and perceptions of sexual harassment and reluctance of the harassed to report their experiences it is difficult to quantify the prevalence of sexual harassment in the workplace and there are some of the studies which have revealed that at the workplace the sexual harassment is considered as the reality for a large number of women.

In the year 2012 there is a survey which is conducted in Australia by the Australian Human Rights Commission, by the name a national telephone survey and which displays that sexual harassment in workplaces in the country was widespread. As per the result there were approximately one in five people aged 15 years and older who were sexually harassed in the workplace in the past five years and one in four women (25%) and one in six men (16%) have been sexually harassed in the workplace in the past five years.

Mostly under the 40 years of age the targets of the sexual harassment were found and it has also been seen that harassers were mostly male co-workers. By a boss or the employer, the survey also indicated that women are at least five times more likely than men to have been harassed. For more than half of all sexual harassment men harassing women accounted for more and while male harassment of men accounted for nearly a quarter.

Between 40% of women experience unwanted sexual advances in the European Union (EU) countries and the physical contact or other forms of sexual harassment at work. In public schools 83% of girls aged 12 to 16 experienced some form of sexual harassment in the United States (U.S.). Across Asia, studies in Japan, Malaysia, the Philippines, and South Korea showed that 30 to 40% of women suffer workplace sexual harassment.

In the year 2011–2012 in India Oxfam India and the Social and Rural Research Institute jointly carried out a study titled Sexual Harassment at Workplaces, which is also covering 400 working women in Delhi, Mumbai, Bangalore, Chennai, Kolkata, Ahmedabad, Lucknow, and Durgapur.

4.2. PREVENTING SEXUAL HARASSMENT

In some of the countries like India, the Sexual Harassment of Women at Workplace (Prevention, Prohibition, and Redressal) Act 2013 deems it the duty of the employer, as well as other responsible persons in work places or institutions to "provide protection against sexual harassment of women at workplace and for the prevention and redressal of complaints of sexual harassment and matters connected therewith or incidental thereto." This implies that these individuals are responsible to:

- Within the workplace prevent or deter the commission of acts of sexual harassment;
- By taking all the required steps there is a need to provide the procedures for the resolution, settlement, or prosecution of acts of sexual harassment (Figure 4.1).

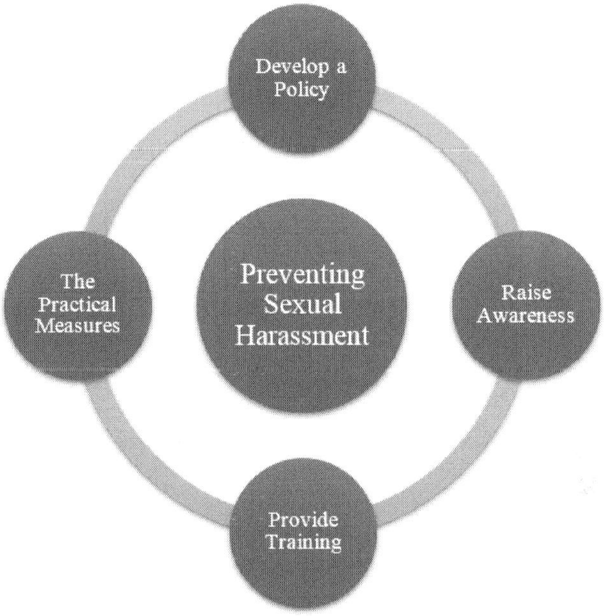

Figure 4.1. Preventing sexual harassment.

Towards the POSH in the workplace the duties of an employer and/or the appropriate Government have been explicitly laid down in the act as follows:

- At the workplace there is a need to provide a safe working environment which shall include safety from third party (outsiders) coming into the contact;
- Display penal consequences of sexual harassment;
- About the grievance handling mechanisms, the information should be displayed and also including about the internal committee;
- At regular intervals organize workshops and awareness programs for sensitizing the employees with the provisions of the act;
- Organize orientation programs for the members of the Internal Committee;
- Under the service rules treat sexual harassment as misconduct and initiate action for such misconduct.
- Moreover, the Act mentions that Government offices will also be responsible for the following:
- To develop relevant IEC (importer-exporter code) and training

materials the Central and State Governments are mandated and to advance the understanding of the public on the provisions of the Sexual Harassment of Women at Workplace (Prevention, Prohibition, and Redressal) Act 2013 organize awareness programs.

- For the members of the Local Complaints Committee (LCC) there is a need for formulation of orientation and training programs.

At the workplace to prevent and address sexual harassment it is vital that employers and organizations take necessary steps in order to implement with strong commitment from leaders and managers. Some of the measures are introduced in subsections.

4.2.1. Develop a Policy

On the prevention of the sexual harassment developing and adopting a comprehensive policy which is one of the key actions in preventing sexual harassment and promoting a safe working environment. At the workplace the aim of such a policy should be to change behavior and attitude of women and men. To provide a workplace environment conducive for both at the workplace.

The contents of a workplace policy on sexual harassment may include:

- On the sexual harassment there is a clear organizations statement:
  - o Sexual harassment is strictly prohibited;
  - o Zero-tolerance policy: For perpetrator in question irrespective of the person's status organization will pursue all sexual harassment cases and not make any exception;
  - o After the investigation if anyone found guilty of sexual harassment will be subject to immediate and appropriate disciplinary action.
- To the sexual harassment key definitions and examples related;
- Reference to relevant legislations;
- Consequences in case of breach of policy;
- Responsibilities of management and staff;
- For regular and repeated training of employees at all levels there should be adequate provisions;
- Details of the members of the Internal Complaints Committee;

- Procedures and options available for getting help and advice, making complaints, and handling cases which can include both formal and informal procedures;
- Procedures and rules for harassment of or by third parties such as clients and customers;
- For redressal procedures there is a timeframe;
- All cases of sexual harassment will be kept confidential and for that there is a clear indication;
- By the management of the institution there are effective safeguards to ensure that the recommendations of the Committee are implemented;
- Frequency of discussion and review of the policy.

About the grievance handling mechanisms there is the display of penal consequences of sexual harassment and information and also including about the Internal Committee are mentioned as duties of employer in Section 19 of the Act.

4.2.2. Raise Awareness

It has been said that employers must raise awareness among employees about the policy and its contents once a policy on sexual harassment is developed, including what constitutes sexual harassment, what an employee can do when he or she experiences sexual harassment, and consequences in case of breach of policy.

Through induction programed of new employees, regular staff meetings or training, email, display on the website, and other appropriate forums this may be done. Moreover, to disseminate information on the anti-sexual harassment policy employers may use visual materials such as notices, posters, or brochures.

There is a need to alert the employees with the provisions of the Act as one of the duties of an employer and/or the appropriate government (Section 19 of the Act). On the sexual harassment policy and its contents, the awareness is raising and to promote the gender equality it is important.

Values are the biggest challenge in the implementation of any law concerning gender equality and women's rights such as the Act on Sexual Harassment and also the experience has shown the patriarchal attitudes. At the workplace in the POSH combating these attitudes are crucial.

4.2.3. Provide Training

For alerting all their staff members the effective training programs are essential and both men and women to recognize sexual harassment to prevent it, and to deal with it when it occurs. To ensure proper understanding and implementation of the organization's policy on sexual harassment the training programmer is the best way.

It is considered as the best forum to communicate to employees and in a non-threatening atmosphere of mutual learning, what behavior is acceptable and what is not. It has been said that training for the members of the Complaints Committee and others who are going to be instrumental in implementing the policy is very essential.

To organize orientation programs for the members of the Internal Committee (Section 19 of the Act) is the duty of an employer. Along with the procedures for taking complaints and enquiry training should include a component on gender sensitization.

For all the employee's sexual harassment training should address perceptions and understanding of sexual harassment, impact of sexual harassment on individuals and workplace, understanding the policy and complaint mechanism.

In addition to these the training for Complaints Committee should address the procedures of investigation, skills necessary for enquiries, documenting the procedures. For the supervisors and managers, a separate training may be organized to encourage appropriate conduct by themselves.

To ensure that the workplace is free from sexual harassment manager plays a key role in promoting the organization's sexual harassment policy. By closely scrutinizing performance and morale of all employees and assessing changes in employee's behavior patterns such as high turnover they also need to monitor the working environment. For the supervisors the training becomes especially important when sexual harassment cases are handled through informal mechanisms.

4.2.4. The Practical Measures

Moreover, employers can take practical actions that can contribute to preventing sexual harassment at workplace to the above-mentioned measures, as follows:

- For all workers to focus on work free from sexual harassment there is a need to create appropriate and safe working environment.

- From the workplace remove offensive, sexually explicit or pornographic calendars, literature, posters, and other materials.
- By ensuring sufficient lighting, open space offices, good balance of men and women at the workplace at different levels there is a need for improving safety of the working environment and during working hours organizing work.
- For making decisions concerning job vacancies or promotions there is a need to establish a panel consisting of both women and men rather than just one individual who is responsible.
- For those who cannot read use images to explain and also translate policy into relevant languages of workers and for sexual harassment display posters about zero-tolerance.
- On sexual harassment distribute brochures on frequently asked questions and answers.
- To identify factors and situations there is a need to conduct surveys which is leading to incidence of sexual harassment. In the past year the survey can be done anonymously and ask employees whether they have experienced any form of sexual harassment.

4.3. PREVENTION OF SEXUAL HARASSMENT (POSH)

Against the sexual harassment the most effective weapon is prevention. On its own, harassment does not disappear. As time goes on it is more likely that when the problem is not addressed, the harassment will worsen and become more difficult to remedy.

4.3.1. Employer Responsibilities

On the employer the burden of preventing sexual harassment rests. Employers are responsible for providing their employees with a work environment that does not discriminate and is free of harassment in the U.S., Canada, and also in some EU Member States. To prevent and deal with harassment in the workplace employers are required by the law to take the steps.

In the workplace the employer has not taken all reasonable steps to prevent and deal with harassment. For any harassment the employer may be liable which does occur, even if unaware that the harassment was taking place. For the sexual harassment a well-articulated standard of employer liability which is committed by an employee.

On the sexual harassment there is most successful preventive strategies and plans it also require the involvement of all those concerned and a clear statement of intent. From all the parties the statement of the intent should reflect a real commitment which is concerned to recognize the importance of the fight against sexual harassment in the workplace. By the establishment of a written policy this is usually accompanied.

All employees that harassment will not be tolerated anti-harassment policies explain what the harassment is and set out how employers and the employees should also respond to the incidents of harassment. When sexual harassment occurs anti-harassment policies should also set forth a detailed mechanism by which employees can make complaints.

There will be no harassment complaints by having an anti-harassment policy which does not mean the same. Therefore, for all staff having an effective policy and procedures which is coupled with the anti-harassment training, it will assist in preventing harassment and support individuals who are being harassed to come forward and ensure that the problem is addressed quickly and effectively.

By taking steps to remedy this, courts have held that an employer who responds quickly and effectively to a complaint and prevents future harassment will not be liable to the same extent, if at all, as an employer who fails to adopt such steps.

In order to create a harassment-free workplace, below there are some of the measures that employers can take which are based on the guidelines from the British Columbia Human Rights Commission Manual Preventing Harassment in the Workplace:

- On a regular basis provide education and information about the harassment to all staff;
- In removing the taboo of silence which often surrounds cases of sexual harassment the circulation of information, open communication and guidance is of particular importance.

So, in this respect information sessions, personnel meetings, office meetings, group discussion and problem-solving groups can prove very effective. With the aggression staff should also be informed to the best way of coping by means of guidelines and staff development programs on sexual harassment at work:

- With the employees, managers, and union representatives there is a need to develop an anti-harassment policy together.

- To all the employees there is a need to communicate the policy.
- To provide a harassment-free work environment it is required to make sure that all managers and supervisors understand their responsibility.
- For dealing with harassment, it has to be made sure that all the employees must understand the policy and the procedures and also the new and long-term employees alike and it also involves training, information, and education.
- It has to be made sure that this policy is being applied to everyone including managers and supervisors.
- Promptly investigate and deal with all complaints of harassment.
- Appropriately discipline employees who harass other employees.
- It has been seen that protection is being provided and support for the employees who feel they are being harassed.
- At the work site take action to eliminate discriminatory jokes, posters, graffiti, e-mails, and photos.
- To ensure that it is still effective for the workplace, it is required to monitor and revise the policy and education/information programs on a regular basis.

For addressing sexual harassment in a confidential and sensitive manner employers should provide a mechanism after a grievance has been filed. Within an organization a well-constructed and well-implemented plan may stop inappropriate conduct before it creates a problem for individual employees or the company.

From the U.S. and Canada many models' anti-harassment policies can be used as sample frameworks for creating systems to prevent workplace harassment in other countries.

4.3.2. Employee Responsibilities

Moreover, to provide a non-discriminatory and non-violent workplace atmosphere is the employers responsibility and employees must also assume an active role in the POSH. Employees should commit to do the following:

- **Understand:**
    - On sexual harassment, obtain, and become familiar with the organizations policy;

- In relation to sexual harassment there is a need to examine one's feelings, attitudes, and behaviors;
- It has been said that there is a need to see that behavior corresponds with the expectations and behavioral requirements of the organizations sexual harassment policy.

- **Observe:**
  - In potential sexual-harassment behaviors or incidents at work be aware and conscious of engaging;
  - By the verbal and non-verbal behavior of others be sensitive to individuals who may be offended;
  - Be aware of subtle forms of sexual harassment;
  - It has been required to watch for and discourage sexual behaviors that negatively affect work.
- **Examine:**
  - In order to avoid unintentional offense, there one must pay attention to the response of others;
  - Nobody should assume that employees or co-workers enjoy or want to hear jokes or sexually oriented comments about their appearance, or be touched, stared at, flirted with, or propositioned for dates or sexual favors;
  - It has been said that if the verbal and nonverbal behaviors might have a negative impact on other co-workers' attitudes toward work then that individual should ask himself;
  - It is required to examine the behavior and gestures of the individual by themselves;
  - It has been said that no one has to take the sexual harassment lightly;
  - Do not take sexual harassment lightly. If you think you are being sexually harassed by an individual or a group, do not accept it as a joke;
  - It has been said that do not encourage the harasser by smiling, laughing at his/her jokes, or flirting back;
  - By the actions let the harasser know that you do not enjoy and do not want this type of attention.
- **Confront:**
  - It has been said that if it is possible, confront the sexual harasser immediately. Tell him/her that this type of attention is offensive;

  - One should tell the harasser that the behavior affects negatively and has the potential of negatively affecting the job if possible;
  - It has been said that one should tell the harasser what behaviors (gestures, physical or verbal) behaviors are offensive, if possible.
- **Resolve:**
  - In order to develop the personal resolution strategy on should seek confidential advice;
  - Consider writing a letter to the harasser and keep a copy;
  - All the incidents of sexual harassment should be documented. About date, time, location, and person/persons involved one should be detailed, precise.
- **Support:**
  - Providing support to the one who is being harassed and also give him or her the support. Encourage the recipient to talk about it and to take immediate action to stop it;
  - To an offensive environment if one could actually see or hear an incident of sexual harassment or are subjected, then can also take the appropriate steps to resolve the harassment or co-file with the complainant;
  - It has been said that when a recipient files a complaint, if possible, support him or her throughout the complaint process.

4.4. DUTIES OF EMPLOYER UNDER PREVENTION OF SEXUAL HARASSMENT (POSH) ACT

At the workplace it has been seen that employees spend more time than their homes and the main thing is that a safe and a comfortable environment is being provided to them where they do not feel threatened or intimidated. At the hands of a colleague or the employer himself, there are numerous factors that can make an employee feel uneasy like workplace discrimination, toxic work environment, lack of code of conduct and sexual harassment.

The barriers of the silence have been broken down by the #MeToo movement and also flooded the Indian news with horror stories of sexual harassment faced by women in an array of sectors including the Bollywood industry, media, MNCs, and even the Indian politics.

An employer has the obligation to provide a safe working environment for women employees under the Sexual Harassment of Women at Workplace

(Prevention, Prohibition, and Redressal) Act, 2013 and at the workplace ensure a swift response in recording and redressing any complaint filed by a woman employee regarding sexual harassment. Under the Posh laws in India there are numerous other responsibilities of an employer. These duties of an employer include the following subsections.

4.4.1. To Establish an Internal Complaints Committee

At the office or branch where at least 10 employees are working an employer must establish an Internal Complaints Committee (ICC). It has been said that if there are no women employees working at present at the establishment an ICC needs to be constituted even.

4.4.2. To Implement a Well-Drafted POSH Policy

It has been said that to put in a place the employer has the obligation and a well-drafted and customized anti-sexual harassment policy, drafted by an experienced employment and labor lawyer in India. From the POSH template policies which are available online a copy-paste policy or a policy copied and would not work as these policies do not meet the actual standards laid down under the POSH Act, 2013 (Figure 4.2).

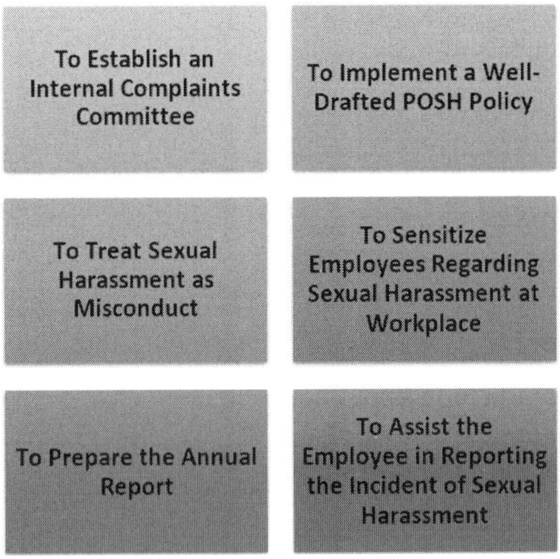

Figure 4.2. Duties of employer under prevention of sexual harassment (POSH) act.

4.4.3. To Treat Sexual Harassment as Misconduct

As misconduct the Anti-Sexual Harassment Act states that any instance of sexual harassment must be treated. The sexual harassment will be treated as misconduct as it is clearly stated by the employment agreements, service rules, policies, and procedures and standing orders. The repercussions of sexual harassment must also be clearly stated like deducting wages, termination of employment, additional penalties, etc.

It has been said that the employer must exhibit the penal consequences of sexual harassment to display the consequences of sexual harassment and at the place of employment the order of the Internal Complaints Committee at a clearly visible place.

4.4.4. To Sensitize Employees Regarding Sexual Harassment at Workplace

To apprise and sensitize employees regarding the issue of sexual harassment all employers have the responsibility. To raise awareness amongst the employees regarding workplace sexual harassment the employers must conduct workshops and organized seminars. It has been said that as per the Central Government rule under the Sexual Harassment Act require the employer to participate in the following activities:

- At the workplace circulate the POSH policy against sexual harassment;
- For members of the Internal Complaints Committee there is a need to execute orientation programs;
- For the ICC members one must conduct capacity and skill-enhancing seminars;
- With Women groups, Panchayati Raj, Local authorities, etc., carry out awareness programs and forums;
- In the POSH policy report the names and details of the ICC members.

4.4.5. To Prepare the Annual Report

To file an annual report regarding the sexual harassment complaints received and their current status it has been said that companies, societies, and trusts are being required. With the Registrar of Companies, the companies registered in India need to file this annual report and with the Charity

Commissioner or Registrar of Societies, societies, and trusts need to file this report. Therefore, sole proprietorships, partnership firms and LLPs (Limited Liability Partnership) do not need to file this annual report, rather, they need to inform the District Officer appointed under the POSH Act about the sexual harassment cases filed with the organization and their status.

4.4.6. To Assist the Employee in Reporting the Incident of Sexual Harassment

In filing a complaint against the accused and helping her in taking a legal action the employer is also responsible to aid the employee and include a criminal measure. It has been said that the employer may also choose to initiate a complaint against the accused if the woman employer desires.

As a violation of the constitutional rights sexual harassment has been held including right to equality, dignity, and personal liberty. in the obliteration the employers of any organization have the key role of even the smallest cases of sexual harassment at workplace and for women employees to work warranting a secure place.

At the workplace the POSH scheme only lays down the minimum standards of protection of women employees from sexual harassment and everything else is up to the employers to their responsibility and making sure that women are not led to the use of the MeToo hashtag.

4.5. SEXUAL HARASSMENT BY SUPERVISORS: WHAT IS IMMEDIATE AND APPROPRIATE CORRECTIVE ACTION?

Issue: In the workforce training that was developed since summer's Supreme Court decisions in Burlington Industries, Inc. v. Ellerth, 118 S. Ct. 2257 (1998), and Faragher v. City of Boca Raton, 118 S. Ct. 2275 (1998), it was emphasized that the company is vicariously liable for unlawful harassment by supervisors. The main importance was on that:

- The company is accountable for the acts of its supervisors as well as for prevention of harassment;
- Employees are responsible for limiting or avoiding the harm from harassment.
- In the training, serious efforts were made to explain that when there is no tangible employment action, the employer may be

able to avoid liability or limit damages by forming an affirmative defense that comprises two imperative elements:

- The employer exercised rational care to avert and correct quickly any harassing behavior; and
- The employee unfairly unsuccessful to take benefits of any corrective or preventive opportunities offered by the employer or otherwise to avoid harm.

The organizers of the training are confident of the preventive measures that have been implemented in developing and enforcing an anti-harassment policy and complaint procedure. But supervisors' questions about what to do if harassment is reported make it clear they do not know what "appropriate and immediate corrective action" means.

Answer: "Immediate and apt corrective action" will eventually be contingent on the specific factual circumstances and, in some instances, the nature of the employer's workforce. Although, here are some guidelines from the EEOC.

4.5.1. Effectiveness

Remedial measures should be designed in such a manner that they help in stopping the harassment, correct its effects on the employee, and make sure that the harassment does not recur. These remedial measures need not be those that the employee appeals or favors, as long as they are effective.

4.5.2. Discipline

In defining discipline, it is important to keep in mind that the employer could be found liable if the harassment does not stop. At the same time, excessively punitive measures may subject the employer to claims such as wrongful discharge and may merely be inapt. To balance these concerns, disciplinary measures should be proportionate to the gravity of the offense.

If the harassment was minor in nature, such as a small number of "off-color" remarks by an individual with no previous history of alike misconduct, then counseling and an oral warning might be all that is essential. While on the other side, if the harassment was persistent or severe in nature, discharge or suspension may be right.

4.6. IMPACT ON COMPLAINANT

Remedial measures should not negatively affect the complainant. Therefore, for instance, if it is imperative to separate the parties, then the harasser should be transferred (unless the complainant prefers otherwise). Remedial responses that penalize the complainant could comprise unlawful retaliation and are not effective in revising the harassment. Remedial measures should be designed in such a manner that it helps in putting the employee in the position he or she would have been in had the misconduct not ensued.

Examples of measures to stop the harassment and ensure that it does not recur:

- Oral or written warning or reprimand;
- Demotion;
- Transfer or reassignment;
- Reduction of wages;
- Discharge;
- Suspension;
- Counseling or training of harasser to make sure that he or she realizes why the conduct violated the employer's anti-harassment policy;
- Monitoring of harassers in order to make sure that harassment stops (Figure 4.3).

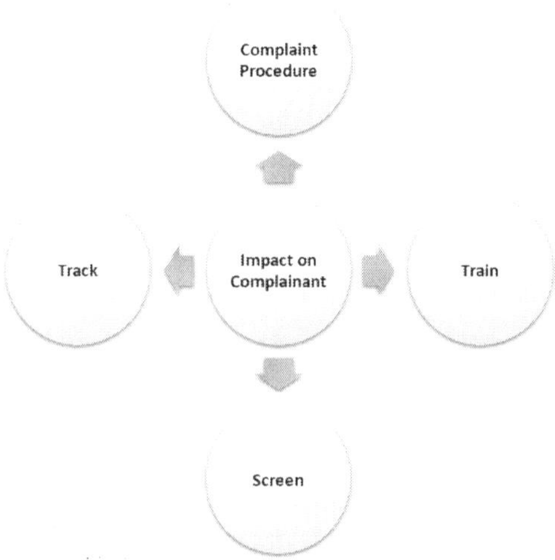

Figure 4.3. Impact on complainant.

Examples of measures to correct the effects of the harassment:

- Restoration of leave taken because of the harassment;
- Expungement of negative evaluation(s) in employee's personnel file that ascended from the harassment;
- Apology by the harasser;
- Reinstatement;
- Monitoring treatment of employee to make sure that he or she is not subjected to retaliation by the harasser or others in the workplace due to the complaint;
- Correction of any other harm instigated by the harassment (e.g., compensation for losses).

4.6.1. Complaint Procedure

Instruct all managers and supervisors to report or address to appropriate officials complaints of harassment, irrespective of whether they are officially chosen to take complaints and regardless of whether a complaint was tricked in a manner that fits to the organization's specific complaint procedures. For instance, if an employee file an EEOC charge asserting unlawful harassment, the employer should commence an internal investigation even if the employee did not complain to management via its internal complaint process.

Moreover, due care needs management to correct harassment irrespective of whether an employee file an internal complaint, if the conduct is evidently unwelcome. If there are areas in the workplace with graffiti containing sexual or racial epithets, management should remove the graffiti, not wait for an internal complaint.

4.6.2. Train

It is essential to make sure that all managers and supervisors recognize their responsibilities under the organization's anti-harassment policy and complaint procedure. Periodic training can assist the company in achieving that result. Such training should explain the sorts of conduct that violate the employer's anti-harassment policy; the gravity of the policy; the responsibilities of managers and supervisors when they learn of alleged harassment; and the prohibition against retaliation.

It is also imperative on part of the employer to keep track of its supervisors' and managers' conduct to make sure that they convey their responsibilities and accountabilities under the organization's anti-harassment program. For instance, an employer could include such compliance in formal evaluations.

4.6.3. Screen

Reasonable preventive measures comprise screening applicants for senior level jobs to see if any have a record of engaging in harassment. If so, it may be essential to reject a candidate based on that or to take additional steps to prevent harassment by that individual.

4.6.4. Track

Lastly, keep records of all complaints of harassment. Without such records, the employer could not be aware of a pattern of harassment by the identical individual. Such a pattern would be pertinent to credibility evaluation and disciplinary measures.

4.7. INSTRUMENTS TO CHECK SEXUAL HARASSMENT

At the regional and the international levels, a range of measures to combat the workplace the sexual harassment has been developed. as a form of sex discrimination and a manifestation of violence against women all of them tend to conceptualize sexual harassment. Some of these instruments are discussed in subsections.

4.7.1. Universal Declaration of Human Rights (UDHR), 1948

In dignity, rights, and freedoms, and equal protection of men and women against any discrimination is being spoken about equality in the Articles 1, 2, and 7.

4.7.2. International Covenant on Economic, Social, and Cultural Rights, 1966

It has been said that without the discrimination of any kind the covenant enjoins all states to guarantee the rights enunciated in it. Between the women and men states must ensure equality for the enjoyment of all economic, social, and cultural rights established in the Covenant. In Article 7 the right to fair conditions of work is enshrined.

4.7.3. United Nations' (UN) Convention on the Elimination of All Forms of Discrimination Against Women (CEDAW), 1979

In the year 1979 the UN Assembly adopted and ratified in the year 1993 by India, and on the ground of sex CEDAW identifies discrimination as a clear violation of Human Rights.

Adopted in 1979 by and ratified in 1993 by India, on the by ratifying the convention, States commit themselves to:

- In their legal system incorporate the equality of men and women and abolishing all discriminatory laws;
- To ensure effective protection of women against discrimination establishing the tribunals and other public institutions;
- Ensuring elimination of all acts of discrimination against women by persons, organizations, or enterprises (Figure 4.4).

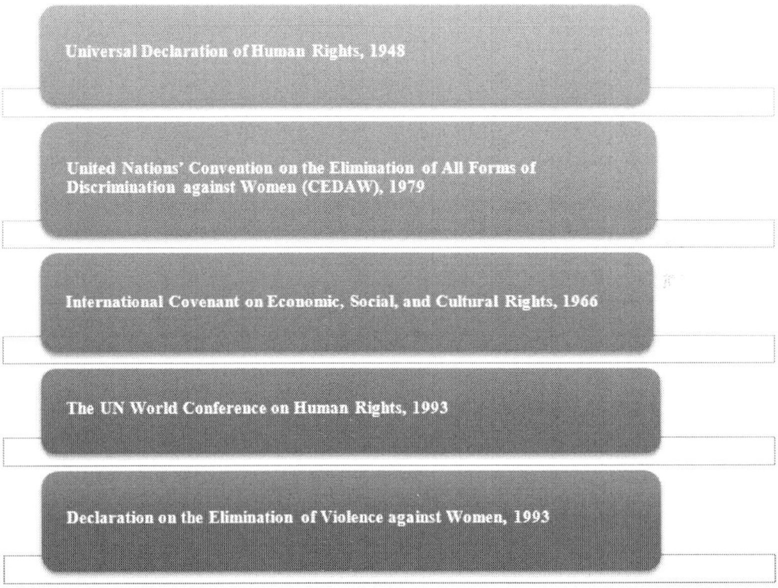

Figure 4.4. Instruments to check sexual harassment.

4.7.4. The UN World Conference on Human Rights, 1993

In the year 1993 this is held in Vienna and as a case of Human Rights violation the UN World Conference on Human Rights identifies sexual harassment and treats it primarily as a form of violence against women.

4.7.5. Declaration on the Elimination of Violence Against Women, 1993

It has been adopted in the year 1993 and to address gender-based violence against women the declaration outlines the steps which states and the United Nations (UN) should take. As any act of the gender-based violence it defines the violence against the women or it is likely to result in, physical, sexual, or psychological harm or suffering to women, including threats of such acts, coercion, or arbitrary deprivation of liberty, whether occurring in public or in private life.

To eliminate any of the custom, tradition, or religious considerations to prevent, investigate it makes clear that states should take the steps and punish the acts of violence against the women in accordance with the national legislation.

4.8. HOW TO STOP SEXUAL HARASSMENT AT THE WORKPLACE: GUIDE FOR EMPLOYERS

Understanding, assessment, sensitivity, and commitment from all quarters is needed by the sexual harassment but it has been said that most importantly from the senior management. It has been said that strong will at the top and a series of well thought out preventive and curative measures, can together ensure sexual harassment free workplace environment. For the employers below a list is given of the recommended measures to express their commitment to end workplace sexual harassment and create a conducive work environment for employees.

Employers should recognize the following: firstly, to provide a sexual harassment free workplace environment for employees is the moral responsibility of the legal system. As, the anxiety and stress produce the impact of sexual harassment can also hit organization's performance and it leads the victim to take time off work due to sickness, reduces efficiency, or forces the victim to leave job.

So, it is important to understand the reason behind the silence of the victim about the sexual harassment. It has been said that an absence of complaints does not necessarily mean an absence of sexual harassment. It may mean that the victims of sexual harassment believe that there is no point in complaining because:

- It will be trivialized;

- The complainant will be subject to ridicule;
- The fear of reprisals (Figure 4.5).

Figure 4.5. How to stop sexual harassment at the workplace: Guide for employers.

4.8.1. Adopt a Sexual Harassment Policy

At the workplace it is an effective measure to prevent the sexual harassment and to adopt a comprehensive sexual harassment policy. The main motive behind this is that the sexual harassment does not occur; and if it occurs, adequate procedure is readily available to deal with problem and prevent its occurrence.

The policy should include:

- To eradicate and prevent sexual harassment an express commitment;
- At the workplace a detailed definition of sexual harassment.

4.8.2. Scope of the Policy

An explanation of penalties:

- In the case of the sexual harassment complaint there is a detailed outline of the procedures of the employees;
- After the investigation there is a clear statement about anyone found guilty of harassment and will be subjected to immediate and appropriate disciplinary action;
- A clear statement and strict rules regarding harassment of or by third parties like clients, customers, etc.;

- For support or consultation additional resource or contact persons available;
- In prevention and complaints resolution an anti-retaliation policy providing protection against retaliation to complaints, witnesses, complaint committee members and other employees involved.

4.8.3. Communicate the Policy and Other Relevant Information

It has been mentioned in the Section 19(b) of Sexual Harassment of Women at Workplace (Prevention, Prohibition, and Redressal) Act, 2013, that there is the requirement of the employer in order to display the penal consequences of sexual harassment at a conspicuous place in workplace. Therefore, at Bulletin Board there should be the display of sexual harassment.

4.8.4. Constitute the Internal Complaint Committee (ICC)

It has been mentioned in the Section 4(b) of the Sexual Harassment of Women at Workplace (Prevention, Prohibition, and Redressal) Act, 2013 that for every employer makes it mandatory to have 10 and more employees to constitute an internal complaint committee (ICC) to deal with cases of sexual harassment.

For the effective resolution of complaints, the employer needs to put down clearly, certain "non-negotiable" for the complaint committee.

- ***Do's:***
  - It has been said that formulize and publicist complaint procedures that are easy and non-threatening;
  - Treat the complaint with respect;
  - Appoint complaints officers-one man and one woman-to serve as the first point of contact;
  - In private most sexual crimes are committed, therefore, there may not be any eyewitnesses;
  - To regain her/his self-respect help the complainant;
  - Always document the results of any sexual harassment complaint or investigation.
- ***Don'ts:***
  - Do not insist on a detailed description of harassment;
  - Do not allow for interruptions when talking to the complainant and/or accused;

- Do not try to determine the impact of the harassment on the complainant;
- Do not discuss the complaint among the presence of the complainant or the accused.

4.8.5. Establish Complaints Channels

To approach the ICC employees, need to be provided different routes and also to file the complaints. As many complaints can be resolved effectively and positively through informal methods, it has been said that informal methods of resolving complaints must be part of the complaint's mechanism.

4.8.6. Workshop/Awareness Program/Training

It has been mentioned in the Section 19(c) of the Sexual Harassment of Women at Workplace (Prevention, Prohibition, and Redressal) Act, 2013, that at regular intervals it is required by the employer to organize workshops and awareness generation programs for sanitizing the employees with the provisions of the Act.

4.8.7. Establish Sensing Mechanism

It has been noted that setting up a mechanism does not mean that there is sexual harassment in the workplace. It has been said that taking prevention is always better and being proactive always helps. In addition to it, change in employees' behavior patterns also deserves the employer's close scrutiny.

4.8.8. Support Internal Complaint Committee (ICC) in Enquiry Process

It has been said that if a company does not enforce them quickly, consistently, and aggressively the most comprehensive sexual policies and procedures are bound to fail. Though, as per the Section 19(d), (e) and (g) require the employer to provide all necessary support to the ICC for dealing with the complaint and conducting an unbiased enquiry.

4.8.9. Encourage Employees and Trade Unions

It has been seen that to combat it speaking out about sexual harassment is an effective tool. The problem has become visible while speaking about it and it is also acknowledged and pushes the management to take effective measures against it. In changing the attitudes of people towards the issue is also being helped after speaking about the sexual harassment. In a diary one must keep track of what happens and also keep any letter or notes or other documents which are being received. Dates, times, places, and an account of what happened should also be written down.

It is necessary to be aware of the situations and also the people who may be harmed. About the particular employee or the social settings, one should not ignore the warnings. For themselves it is required to acknowledge their concern.

The employer should also encourage the trade union to:

- To realize that sexual harassment is a major problem which cannot be simply ignored to help the employees.
- By talking to the harasser try to informally resolve the complaint first. If that is ineffective, file a complaint with the appropriate authority to help the victim.
- About the issue, educate the members.
- In the workplace, determine the extent of the problem. It has been said that a survey of the members may be useful.
- To jointly conduct training program work with employers.
- Try to stop any harassment they observe, whether or not the victim has complained.
- To protect the confidentiality of all who are involved disclose information only to the extent necessary.

4.9. PREVENTING AND RESPONDING TO SEXUAL HARASSMENT

For maintain an environment the ultimate responsibility is free from sexual harassment rests with employers, housing providers, educators, and other responsible parties covered by the Code. It is not acceptable to choose to stay unaware of sexual harassment from a human rights perspective, whether or not a human rights claim has been made.

In the Ontario organizations and institutions operating have a legal duty to take steps to prevent and respond to breaches of the Code, including sexual harassment. It has to be made sure that the employers, housing providers, educators, and other responsible parties must make sure they maintain poison-free environments that respect human rights. So, this requires commitment and work which is also worth it.

There is the violation of the code by the employers, housing providers, educators, and other responsible parties where they directly or indirectly, intentionally, or unintentionally infringe the Code, or where they do not directly infringe the Code but authorize, condone, or adopt behavior that is contrary to the Code.

To condone or further a discriminatory act there is a clear human rights duty not to condone or that has already happened. The life of the initial discriminatory act is being continued or extended. Through the contractual relations or in other ways this duty extends to people who, while not the main actors, are drawn into a discriminatory situation.

For the action of third parties such as customers, contractors, etc., who engage in sexually harassing behavior which depends on the circumstances, employers, housing providers, educators, and other responsible parties may be held liable for the actions of third parties.

On the organization's failure human rights decision-makers often find organizations liable, and assess damages to respond appropriately to address discrimination and harassment. About the individuals' instances of discrimination or harassment an organization may respond to the complaints, if the underlying problem is not resolved they may still be found to have not responded appropriately.

Apart from the punishing the individual harasser there may be a poisoned environment, or an organizational culture that condones sexual harassment. In these cases, organizations must take further steps, such as training and education, to better address the problem. It has been said that an organization has a legal duty to respond to a complaint of sexual harassment, and may be found liable for not doing so, even where the complaint is ultimately not made out.

At the time of deciding whether an organization has met its duty to respond to human rights claim there are some things which are to be considered:

- At the time to deal with discrimination and harassment procedures should be in place;
- The promptness of the organization's response to the complaint;
- How seriously the complaint was treated;
- To deal with the complaint mad the resources available;
- For the person who complained whether the organization provided a healthy environment;

- To the person who complained how well the action taken was communicated.

On developing the human rights policies and the procedures the guidelines are being entitled in its publication and to help organizations meet their human rights obligations the OHRC (Ontario Human Rights Commission) provides more information and take proactive steps to make sure their environments are free from discrimination and harassment.

4.9.1. Anti-Sexual Harassment Policies

For promoting a harassment-free environment for individuals protected by the Code by having a clear, comprehensive anti-sexual harassment policy in place employers, housing providers, educators, and other responsible parties can go a long way toward.

The policy will alert all parties to their rights, roles, and responsibilities in the cases of alleged sexual harassment. It has been said that policies must be clearly set out that how the sexual harassment will be dealt with promptly and efficiently.

It has been said that for resolving complaints everyone should be aware of the existence of an anti-sexual harassment policy and the steps in place.

This can be done by giving policies to everyone as soon as they are introduced. By including the policies in any orientation material making all employees, tenants, students, etc., aware of them.

On human rights issues training people, including people in positions of responsibility, on the contents of the policies, and providing ongoing education.

Harm and the liability can get reduced by an effective sexual harassment policy. The equity and diversity goals of organizations are also being promoted and also makes good business sense.

For dealing with sexual harassment by third parties' employers, housing providers, educators, and other responsible parties also need procedures. To respond to the harassment these procedures should show how people are expected and also make sure that serious and/or ongoing problems are brought to the attention of those in charge, and also that the people in charge take appropriate steps to assess the situation and take remedial action.

It is very important that all complaints of sexual harassment be taken seriously and dealt with promptly in practice. In order to be disciplined or reprisal the complaint mechanism be applied, and that persons making complaints not be subjected. To make sure they are free of sexually harassing behaviors all responsible parties should monitor their environments regularly. There is a need for the proactive steps in order to maintain a poison-free environment will help make sure that sexual harassment does not take root, and is not given a chance to escalate.

Suggested contents of an anti-sexual harassment policy:

- To maintain a fair and equitable environment free of sexual and gender-based harassment a vision statement setting out the organization's commitment, and stating that the organization will not tolerate sexual and gender-based harassment.
- Under the Ontario Human Rights Code, a statement of rights and obligations.
- In the Code a list of the prohibited grounds of discrimination listed.
- The Code definition of "sexual harassment" and a definition of "gender-based harassment."
- As a violation of the Code there is an explanation of the concept of a poisoned environment, and examples of a poisoned environment that are meaningful in that organization's context.
- A description of unacceptable behavior, such as:
- In the OHRC's Policy the examples of sexual harassment as listed on preventing sexual and gender-based harassment.
- A description of who the policy applies to (such as employers, employees, third party service providers, etc.).
- With details on how internal complaints will be handled:
  - who to complain to;
  - an assurance that the person handling the complaint should be independent, expert, etc.;
  - confidentiality;
  - reassurance that the person making the complaint will be protected from reprisal, or threat of reprisal;
  - For parties to a complaint, help that is available;
  - To resolve a complaint the availability of Alternative Dispute Resolution, such as mediation;
  - How the complaint will be investigated;

  - How long the process will take;
  - Steps that will be taken if it is not appropriate for the person making the complaint to continue working with the person/people being complained about;
  - When the harasser is unknown how the organization will deal with the complaint (e.g., cyber harassment).
- If the claim of sexual harassment is proven remedies that will be available, such as:
  - Disciplinary measures to be applied (for example, in employment, measures could range from a verbal warning or a letter of reprimand to termination);
  - Compensation to the person who made the complaint.
- To file other types of complaints a statement reinforcing the right of individuals, such as:
  - With the Human Rights Tribunal of Ontario (HRTO), a human rights application at any time during the internal process, as well as an explanation of the one-year time limit in the Code;
  - A complaint under the Occupational Health and Safety Act, if applicable;
  - A grievance under a collective agreement, if applicable;
  - Criminal charges, if applicable.

4.9.2. Employers

To ensure a poison-free work environment is the duty of the employers and in their workplace take steps to make sure that sexual harassment is not taking place. To remedy this situation employers must take immediate action once they learn of sexual harassment. When the harassment has happened and if the employer is satisfied, they must consider both disciplinary action and further prevention steps, such as training or education.

It has been mentioned under the 46.3 of the Code, a corporation, trade union or occupational association, unincorporated association or employers' organization will be held responsible for discrimination, including acts or omissions, committed by employees or agents in the course of their employment. For the discrimination arising there are displaced liability may make an employer responsible from the acts of its employees or agents, done in the normal course, whether or not it had any knowledge of, participation in, or control over these actions. With the harassment Vicarious liability does not apply to breaches of the sections of the Code dealing. Therefore, when harassment amounts to or results in a poisoned environment the existence of a poisoned environment is a form of discrimination as per the Section 46.3 of the Code will apply.

It has been said that the organic theory of the corporate liability in these cases may also apply. An organization may be liable for acts of harassment carried out by its employees if it can be proven that it was aware of the harassment, or the harasser is shown to be part of the management or "directing mind" of the organization under this theory. For the decisions, acts, or omissions of the employee in such cases an organization will be liable:

- It has been said that the employee who is part of the "directing mind" engages in harassment or inappropriate behavior that violates the Code;
- It has been noted that the employee who is part of the "directing mind" does not respond adequately to harassment or inappropriate behavior they are aware of, or should reasonably be aware of.

In an organization managers and central decision-makers are part of the "directing mind." All the people who are having the supervisory authority may also be the part of the directing mind, if they act, or are seen to act, as representatives of the organization. If they in effect have supervisory authority or significant responsibility for guiding employees even non-supervisors may be considered part of the directing mind.

4.9.3. Housing Providers

To make sure that housing providers must take the proactive steps that sexual harassment does not take place on their premises. To intervene and respond appropriately they must take immediate steps, if the sexual harassment happens. Between housing providers and female tenants there is often dramatic power imbalance for example, may mean that women may not report sexual harassment due to fear of retribution, being evicted, or concerns about their physical safety, the safety of their families and/or their personal belongings. It has been mentioned earlier that a corporation, trade union or occupational association, unincorporated association or employers' organization will be held responsible for discrimination, including acts or omissions, committed by employees or agents in the course of their employment under Section 46.3 of the Code.

In housing this known as vicarious liability and it also applies to human rights violations. Example, to a young female tenant a contracted maintenance worker repeatedly makes lewd comments. The landlord has a duty to promptly address the worker's conduct and to make sure the living environment is poison-free.

For discrimination or harassment arising from the acts of its employees or agent's vicarious liability may make a housing provider responsible, done in the normal course, whether or not it had any knowledge of, participation in, or control over these actions.

It has been said that in these types of cases the organic theory of the corporate liability may also be applied. It has been said that if it can be proven that it was aware of the harassment an organization may be liable for acts of harassment carried out by its employees under this theory or the harasser is shown to be part of the management or "directing mind" of the organization. For the decision, acts, or omissions of the employee an organization will be liable in such types of cases.

- In harassment or inappropriate behavior that violates the Code the employee who is part of the "directing mind" engages;
- The employee who is part of the "directing mind" does not respond adequately to harassment or inappropriate behavior they are aware of, or should reasonably be aware of.

4.10. CONCLUSION

This chapter gives an insight to the reader about the organizational responsibility to prevent, prohibit, and redress sexual harassment at the workplace. It talks about the measures in order to prevent harassment such as developing policy, spreading awareness, providing training, and the various other practical measures.

It throws light on the two aspects that is the employer responsibilities and employer responsibility which plays a major role in the prevention of the sexual harassment. It highlights the duties of employer under POSH act which deals with the establishment of internal complaints committee. Implementing well drafted policies, treating sexual harassment as a misconduct, preparing annual report, etc.

This chapter also provides an overview on the instruments used so as to check sexual harassment, that is the UDHR, the UN world conference on human rights, declaration on the elimination of violence against women.

As the chapter proceeds, it discusses the measures to stop sexual harassment at the workplace by outlining the policies and their scope, workshop, awareness, and strategies, establishing complaints channels and sensing mechanism, etc., along with putting emphasis upon the preventing and responding to sexual harassment which deals with employers and housing providers.

REFERENCES

1. (2020). Prevention of Sexual Harassment at the Workplace (POSH) Legal and HR Considerations. [eBook] Nishith Desai Associates. Available at: https://www.nishithdesai.com/fileadmin/user_upload/pdfs/ (accessed on 17 August 2021).
2. (n.d.). The Sexual Harassment of Women at Workplace (Prevention, Prohibition, and Redressal) Act-2013. [eBook] Available at: https://legislative.gov.in/sites/default/files/A2013-14.pdf (accessed on 17 August 2021).
3. HR Library, (2003). Sexual Harassment-Prevention of Sexual Harassment. [Online] Hrlibrary.umn.edu. Available at: http://hrlibrary.umn.edu/svaw/harassment/explore/5prevention.htm (accessed on 17 August 2021).
4. Ontario Human Rights Commission, (2021).8. Preventing and Responding to Sexual Harassment | Ontario Human Rights Commission. [Online] Ohrc.on.ca. Available at: http://www.ohrc.on.ca/en/policy-preventing-sexual-and-gender-based-harassment/8-preventing-and-responding-sexual-harassment-0 (accessed on 17 August 2021).
5. Shivi, (2018). Duties of Employer Under Prevention of Sexual Harassment (POSH) Act | Legistify. [Online] Legistify.com. Available at: https://www.legistify.com/blogs/view_detail/duties-of-employer-under-prevention-of-sexual-harassment-act/ (accessed on 17 August 2021).
6. Tine, S., (2013). Preventing and Responding to Sexual Harassment at Work: Guide to the Sexual Harassment of Women at Workplace. [eBook] New Delhi, India. Available at: https://www.ilo.org/wcmsp5/groups/public/---asia/---ro-bangkok/---sro-new_delhi/documents/publication/wcms_630227.pdf (accessed on 17 August 2021).

Chapter 5

Anti-Sexual Harassment Training

CONTENTS

In the chapter anti sexual harassment training, current status and need for training in prevention of "sexual harassment" at work is discussed. It also highlighted how can training prevent or reduce "sexual harassment" at the workplace. It also explained benefits of conduct anti sexual harassment trainings for companies. In addition, it also shed some light on some of the most important ways in which training can prevent or reduce "sexual harassment" at the workplace. It also discussed the role of training in managing complaints. It also demonstrates when it is essential to conduct such training programs. Furthermore, it also explains how to make sure that the company's "anti-sexual harassment" training is effective.

Moreover, it also tries to explain how to report an allegation of sexual harassment, harassment, discrimination, and/or retaliation information about retaliation. At the end, it discussed some of the challenges of harassment training and grievance procedures.

5.1. INTRODUCTION

It is observed that since past few years, there has been increase in awareness and acknowledgement that "Sexual Harassment" does exist and is widely predominant at the workplace. There have been various measures that have been introduced at the workplace by employers' Governments, and workers' associations all over the world.

Legislations, awareness campaigns, training, and counseling of employees have been some of the measures that helps in addressing and preventing "Sexual Harassment" at the workplace. The objective of this chapter is to highlight how training employees and employers can help in the prevention of "Sexual Harassment" at the workplace. Training in this chapter here refers to training people from the following categories:

- Employees in general: about awareness, complaints, and consequences;
- Victims in specific: about how to raise complaints, the party to whom to approach, their rights, etc.;
- Employers: about handling such behavior, prevention measures, ensuring a "safe" workplace and how to handle and address different categories of complaints;
- Internal Complaint Committee (IC or ICC) members-Steps in handling complaints, using attitude and tact needed, creating a conducive environment for the victim to come out courageously.

With the workforce becoming gradually diverse, a number of ethical issues crop up at work. One of the major challenges is sexual harassment at the place of work. "Sexual Harassment" is portrayed by annoying sexual advances, gestures, communications, and other acts intended at others.

The addressee feels that these actions are a violation of their rights and impede their work. The outcome of a survey conducted by SHRM in 2018 (Society for Human Resource Management (SHRM), 2018) brought out a serious, shocking fact where organizations have logged an increase in the number of "Sexual Harassment" complaints over the past two years. It was observed that both female and male employees had complained of sexual harassment.

Around 37% of the companies who had participated in the survey asserted that they had some sort of training given every year to employees about "Sexual Harassment" at the workplace. 8% of the organizations had plans to train and inform their employees about such an issue in the coming year.

Around 25% of the organizations professed that there had been a consistent increase in the number of complaints about "Sexual Harassment" being filed, in the recent few years.

According to the ILO, "Sexual Harassment," particularly when it happens at the place of work, becomes an obstacle in the way of offering safe and decent environment for all its employees. Research has specified that the scale of the problem of "Sexual Harassment" at the workplace has augmented significantly due to the ineffectual policies, lack of commitment among managers and untrained manpower to deal with cases of workplace sexual harassment (Sharma, 2010).

According to a survey conducted in 2018, by SHRM (2018), it was stated that reports that though 94% of the respondents say that their company has a policy in place to safeguard its employees against "Sexual Harassment," and 72% of the employees in the US, are pleased with the company's attempt to avert harassment, yet more than 1/3 of them believe that their workplace provides several opportunities and situations for harassment.

The survey further brings out that constant awareness programs can teach the team about behaviors that are correct, and which behaviors should be evaded at the workplace.

Sharyn Potter, Kristin Smith, and Jane Stapleton examined the data presented by the Granite State Poll in 2018 (Kristin, 2019). The report specifies that more than 50% of the women and at least 25% of the men in New Hampshire have witnessed some kind of "sexual harassment" or the other at their place of work. The predominance of such incidents of Sexual harassment across the world signify that, sexual harassment is not restricted to any one specific culture or country. The "#MeToo1" movement that has caught momentum like a raging inferno has brought many skeletons tumbling out of several unlikely closets.

Though validity of all cases has not and cannot be recognized, such situations push the case for greater awareness programs with respect to what acts could be construed as "Sexual Harassment." Several cases that have stemmed from "lack of awareness" and "ignorance" by the organization, the survivor or the perpetrator could have been evaded if structured training or awareness programs (on how to file complaints, how to handle complaints as well as malicious complaints) had been conducted.

5.1.1. Key Factors That Make Sexual Harassment Prevention Training Crucial

- ***Employees are Protected*:** It is generally seen that having a zero-tolerance policy and ensuring adequate training empowers your employees and makes them feel comfortable at work. It allows them to feel secure and protected in the company and thus having a good environment in the company.
- ***Training Helps Improve Morale*:** Taboo, as it might sound, the issue of sexual harassment must be addressed head-on. Sexual harassment prevention training through robust HR Services ensures that an organization's employees feel more committed and confident. It helps in working towards the goal of organization by eliminating negativity in the company.
- ***Companies are Protected from Legal Liability*:** It is generally seen that by providing regular training, sexual harassment at the workplace can be reduced greatly. This results in reduced legal liability for the companies. Investing a little amount on training can help in saving millions if the company is being sued.
- ***Employee Productivity Increases*:** Providing effective training with professional HR Training and Consultancy helps the employees in getting the feeling of more value. This results in making the employees a more committed workforce that warrants the most optimal productivity.

- ***The Expected Behavior is Achieved*:** It is generally seen that training imparts culture and discipline. Standardized training conducted by expert HR Services will help in ensuring HR Compliance and defines and develops acceptable behavior among employees of the company.

Employers can avoid legal as well as financial liabilities by arranging effective sexual harassment prevention training at regular intervals provided by expert HR Services. Training ensures HR Compliance while empowering and educating employees. Furthermore, one can also make sure a better organizational culture wherein everyone understands the expected and accepted behavior.

5.2. NEED FOR TRAINING IN PREVENTION OF "SEXUAL HARASSMENT" AT WORK AND CURRENT STATUS

It is worth noticing that there has been several researches and reports have put forward the fact that incidences of "Sexual Harassment" at workplaces are not new and that debates have been going around how to address this menace since the 1970s (Figure 5.1).

Figure 5.1. Formulation of anti-sexual harassment training procedures in the workplace.

Source: Image by Online Course Bay.

Internationally, it has been noticed as a kind of violence and discrimination against women. Since the late 1990s, countries have been actively working towards coming out with particular legal measures based on which they can declaring that "Sexual Harassment" is a criminal and civil offence.

The ILO report emphasizes that employers are being regarded as responsible for the enforcement of such legal measures at the workplace through formulation of policies to avert sexual harassment.

The employer cannot relinquish his responsibility or accountability in making the workplace a safe and better place to work. Just as he is accountable if any accident takes place, he is also liable in case an incident of "Sexual Harassment" occurs.

Thus, employers are obliged to design Anti "Sexual Harassment" policies on the basis of the Government framework, create awareness and make sure that these policies are applied. The employer is also needed to produce an environment where the victim does not hesitate to voice or raise his/her complaint.

Employees, Employers organizations, and NGOs are designing sample policies, directing organizations on compliance and carrying out training and research activities. Nonetheless, the onus of alerting employees about the issue of "Sexual Harassment" depends on the employer, so that incidences of "Sexual Harassment" at the workplace can be averted.

Though Anti "Sexual Harassment" training of employees is not statutory, several countries have integrated the clause in the laws where particular training regarding sexual training is compulsory. For instance, in India, Prevention of "Sexual Harassment" at the Workplace, commonly recognized as POSH, is founded on a statute passed in December 2013.

Chapter VIII, Section 19 of the act makes it obligatory for the employer to "organize workshops and conduct awareness programs at regular intervals for sensitizing the employees with the provisions of the Act and orientation programs for the members of the internal Committee in the manner as may be prescribed" (Ministry of Women and Child Development, GOI, 2013).

The main objective of this is that no one can claim "ignorance" as an excuse. This Act needs every company to form an Internal Complaint Committee (ICC). The aim of this committee receives and enquires into any complaints with respect to "Sexual Harassment" in the organization.

It is obligatory that the ICC members must be trained enough to deal with different types of complaints and be fully aware of the procedure to look into such matters, which are referred to them. In addition to this, the Act has also emphasized upon the Government role, and said that wherever possible, the Government must provide enough training materials, awareness workshops as well as measure to create awareness on how to deal with the prevention of this menace as well as how to handle complaints.

In a survey conducted by E&Y in 2015, it was found that 21% of the respondents' organizations had not steered any awareness campaigns for its employees in relation to sexual harassment. 44% of the employees who responded uttered that they were not aware of the penal consequences of "Sexual Harassment" and neither had their organization put up any posters or sign, etc., regarding the same (EY Forensic and Integrity Services, 2015).

Amongst the 27% of the MNCs surveyed and 50% of the SMEs which answered to the survey had not conducted any training for their ICC members. In addition, the survey exposed that across all sectors there was very meagre or no training conducted for employees particularly for the new employees.

It was also publicized that even in IT companies, 46% of the companies have not employed their IT expertise to offer online modules to create awareness amongst newcomers (EY Forensic and Integrity Services, 2015).

5.3. HOW CAN TRAINING PREVENT OR REDUCE "SEXUAL HARASSMENT" AT THE WORKPLACE?

It is generally seen that majority of the employers develop well worded policies with respect to anti-sexual harassment. Research has though suggested that employers opine that their responsibilities start and end with executing a policy onto the organization as well as setting up the compulsory (Haspels, 2001; Dang, 2017; Sharma, 2010).

Several organizations develop an anti-sexual harassment policy. Although, it can be seen that employers adopt an almost indifferent attitude towards sexual harassment and thus assume their responsibilities end with preparing a policy and setting up the mandatory ICC that is a must as per the act.

They do not identify that training can offer the vital bridge between the anti-sexual harassment policies and attained positive outcomes. In short, employers must understand that even the best policy, without training assistance, would remain nothing but a paper tiger (Lindenberg, 2003). Thus, the responsibility of an employer with respect to the "Sexual Harassment of Women at Workplace Act, 2013," is not just to set up a complaint committee but to make sure that the employees are aware of the ways to seek redressal, how to raise a complaint, and comprehend the penal provisions under the act. All these have made awareness and training sessions the need of the hour, so that employees comprehend the law and the results of violation and non-conformity.

Employers or employees can no longer claim unfamiliarity when they are faced with cases of sexual harassment. It is generally seen that "Sexual Harassment" is more likely to arise in workplace environments that tolerate bullying, yelling, innuendo, intimidation, and other forms of discourteous behavior (Orser, 2000).

Going beyond just the mandatory training, the employer should invest adequate time and resources in interventions that change the mind-set of employees concentrating on inclusion and gender sensitivity.

Training employees not to be mute bystanders through such interventions and supporting victims to complain courageously would help to create an atmosphere where people recognize they cannot get away easily after sexually harassing a colleague (Kristin, 2019).

5.4. BENEFITS OF CONDUCT ANTI-SEXUAL HARASSMENT TRAININGS FOR COMPANIES

For years, experts in the fields of economics, sociology, and medicine have explored on the ill-effects of sexual harassment at the workplace. Several countries have laws to stop and redress acts of sexual harassment in the workplace. Irrespective of such efforts, several companies fail to avert sexual harassment in the workplace because of their failure to conduct Anti-Sexual Harassment Training for their employees (Figure 5.2).

Figure 5.2. Sexual harassment in the workplace.

Source: Image by Pixabay.

The #MeToo and Time's Up movements in current few times have shown that instances of sexual harassment in the workplace can stain a company's public image as well as goodwill and prompt a loss of confidence in employees about how safe the workspace is for them.

Anti-sexual harassment training (hereby, 'ASH training') is considered as one of the most imperative an employer can do to stop harassment and other inappropriate conduct in the workplace. 5 key reasons why company should conduct ASH training are discussed as in subsections.

5.4.1. Reduces Legal and Financial Liability

The Sexual Harassment of Women at Workplace (Prohibition, Prevention, and Redressal) Act, 2013, commonly recognized as the POSH Act, places a duty on the employer to organize awareness programs and workshops at regular intervals for alerting the employees with the provisions of the Act. This exercise is a legal obligation and failure to comply with the same will result in a fine that may extend to jail.

Companies that are repeat offenders can be penalized twice as much as they were for the previous offense, and could even be subject to the cancellation of any licenses, permits or registrations that they may need to undertake their business. While the penalty for the first offence under the POSH Act might not be a heavy one for a large company, getting licenses and registrations revoked for repeated offenses can result in huge losses and burdensome to the offender-company.

Losses accrued from halted operations mingled with the costs and time related in re-applying for a license or registration can total up to an extremely large amount. Regularly conducting ASH training could help avert this.

5.4.2. Ensures Employees Feel Safe at Work and Are Able to Be Productive

Being subject to or witness to sexual harassment in the workplace can be a disturbing experience and can take a toll on the witness/victim's' physical and mental health. The more individuals encounter sexual harassment in the workplace, the more likely they report symptoms of depression, anxiety, and stress. This is also followed by a general impairment of psychological well-being.

A study conducted in the U.S. found that 1 in 5 self-identified sexual harassment victims met the criteria for a DSM-IV diagnosis of Major Depressive Disorder, and 1 in 10 described symptoms steady with Post Traumatic Stress Disorder (PTSD).

This can have a huge impact on the performance of individuals in the workplace and result in amplified costs for organization because of reduced productivity and commitment (Pearson et al., 2000).

According to a study conducted by Deloitte in Australia in the year 2018, workplace sexual harassment levied a number of costs-$2.6 billion in lost productivity (or $1,053 on average per victim) and $0.9 billion in other costs (or $375 on average per victim).

At an average weekly wage of $1,244 across the Australian economy, each case of workplace sexual harassment resulted in adequately four working days of lost output. The study also disclosed the huge losses that stemmed from absenteeism-28% of total costs were because of an employee's failure to report for or remain at work as scheduled, because of the fear and discomfort instigated by sexual harassment in the workplace.

In Deloitte's study, workplaces having a greater number of instances of workplace harassment also suffered from higher employee turnover rates.

This can be endorsed to the earlier mentioned psychological side-effects of workplace harassment. Staff turnover contributed the greatest to productivity loss and associated costs amounted to the 32% of the total costs of sexual harassment in the workplace.

While these surveys were not undertaken in developing countries, they provide a fair idea about the impact sexual harassment has on workplace productivity.

It is generally seen that conducting regular anti-sexual harassment training makes the workplace safer, assuages the discomfort and fears of employees, augments employee satisfaction, lessens employee turnover and saves companies from the massive costs related with lower productivity.

5.4.3. Information on the Legal Rights of Someone Accused of Sexual Harassment

While a major proportion of anti-sexual harassment training is emphasized on the prevention and redressal of sexual harassment of employees in the workplace, effective ASH training also teaches employees about their legal rights if they are alleged of sexual harassment.

Every employee alleged under the POSH Act is afforded certain rights by the Act that assists in safeguarding the accused's interests. This is imperative information since most sexual harassment redressal proceedings are steered without the existence of legal counsel.

Being aware of one's rights can avert wrongful convictions and lengthy legal battles. Employees are also well-informed about the redressal procedure, and trained to point out wrong practices during an IC proceeding. In addition, employees are made aware of their rights if they are deceptively accused of sexual harassment.

Anti-sexual harassment training ensures that the POSH Act and its facilities are not used as a tool of retribution to settle scores, and that employees are safeguarded from false complaints.

This training also ranges to educating the IC (Internal Committee) members on the best redressal practices. While a complaint of sexual harassment is not redressed in a court-like environment, the IC proceedings are still quasi-judicial in nature.

This needs IC members to comprehend the principles of natural justice, ensure that IC proceedings are unprejudiced, maintain privacy of all complaints, and make sure that individuals are not held guilty before an in-depth investigation finds them guilty of the acts they are being suspected of.

5.4.4. Communicates That the Workplace Has Zero-Tolerance for Sexual Harassment

While, it is often seen that most companies today boast of a 'zero tolerance for sexual harassment' policy, it is challenging to ensure that the company's workplace has zero tolerance without anti-sexual harassment training.

Anti-sexual harassment training teaches employees about what sort of conduct constitutes sexual harassment, educates them how to file a complaint, inspires employees to report any dubious behavior that makes them feel uncomfortable, sensitizes higher-level and managers staff on matters pertaining to sexual harassment, educates IC member about the procedure of complaints and trains bystanders on how to interfere if they are experience to sexual harassment. All of these elements come together to produce a workplace that has zero tolerance for sexual harassment.

Undertaking periodic and rigorous anti-sexual harassment training also directs out a strong message from the top to the workforce that the Company is taking a robust stand against sexual harassment.

5.4.5. Makes All Kinds of Workplaces Safer

The POSH Act expands the definition of the term 'workplace' to comprise any place a woman employee calls out of or during the course of employment. This also embraces transportation offered by an employer for the objective of commuting to and from the place of employment. Although, most employees are ignorant about this concept of an 'extended workplace.'

This, in addition with the fact that most employees are needed to visit a diverse set of locations and venues during the course of their employment results in most examples of sexual harassment outside the official workplace go unreported. These locations endure to remain unsafe for employees since the IC is incapable of taking any action against the perpetrators.

Anti-sexual harassment training particularly emphasizes on educating employees about the concept of an 'extended workplace' and inspires them to report instances of sexual harassment outside of the official place of work.

When examples of sexual harassment are stated, the IC and the company can take action against the suspect, thus, making these locations harmless for anyone who visits. It also means that non-official work environments, such as a work-from-home environment are made better by bringing them within the IC's jurisdiction.

5.5. SOME OF THE MOST IMPORTANT WAYS IN WHICH TRAINING CAN PREVENT OR REDUCE "SEXUAL HARASSMENT" AT THE WORKPLACE

5.5.1. Create Awareness

Awareness can help in the number of ways that are discussed as follows:

- ***Curtailment of such behaviors which may be viewed as "sexual" and punishable*:** When the author described 20 behaviors/acts to women and men, there were about 9 acts which both viewed as offensive or unsuitable, while there were 14 acts which only women noticed as offensive.
- There is clear evidence that amongst many men, there is a lack of awareness and a gap amongst the understanding between both men and women as to how to make several gestures. actions could be viewed. For instance, placing an arm around a woman could be considered as a sexually intimidating gesture by the woman. When awareness is produced that certain acts are those which could be labeled as "sexual harassment" males may desist from such acts.
- ***Awareness of how to react in such situations*:** In the unfortunate circumstances if such an event/act occurs, the victim must know whom to criticize and what should be his/her reaction. Such awareness would help in creating an environment where the victim is expedited to speak fearlessly. This in turn would ring a bell of caution to prevent/stall any other further such incidents.
- ***Awareness to the Employer*:** The employer should also become aware of how to handle such situations, how to design tangible policies and how to execute them. It helps in legal compliance. Employers should be well aware that it is not just the aggressor who is accountable for punishment.

If the victim can prove that the employer did not have the adequate mechanism in place to avert and redress "sexual harassment" complaints, the employer is also liable for punishment. Added to this would be the damage it could cause to the reputation and goodwill of the company.

5.5.2. Enhancing Diversity Management

The employee of today is required to move away from narrow, conservative thinking to broader, inclusive mind-sets. Whatever his personal views on gender, dressing, sexual orientation, etc., he cannot carry them to the workplace and endanger the workplace. With a greater number of LGBT's at the workplace, sensitization of employees is extremely imperative.

It is important to understand that our team mates may be wholly different from us in several ways and stop being judgmental. Thus, training regarding diversity should comprise anti "Sexual Harassment" training.

Teasing or ridiculing people because they are transgender, gays or lesbians are regarded as acts of "Sexual Harassment" globally. Diversity and "Sexual Harassment" training must go hand in order to create an inclusive organization.

5.6. HOW TRAINING CAN HELP IN MANAGING COMPLAINTS?

The POSH Act has specified certain conditions for an employer to comply with. One imperative need is the formation of an ICC (Supreme Court of India, 2013).

This is the body that is supposed to receive and handle the complaints from the woman and conduct queries with respect to the norms laid down in the Act as well as the company policy. Any organization having 10 or more than those employees must have an ICC that has been set up by the employer.

The names of these members have to be obviously displayed at prominent places of the organizations. The ICC usually constitutes of:

- A chairperson, who is a senior women employee in the organization;
- Two women employees-who have information about the law and are dedicated to the cause of women;
- One external member from an NGO or any woman who is fervent about the cause of women.

While the explanation of the qualifications of the members of the ICC is extremely vague in the act, it is very transparent in the Act that the ICC is mandatory. As demonstrated from the case at Novasoft technologies the absence of a Complaints Committee or an ICC defies the fundamental right of the woman to a free and fair working place. (Ms. G v. ISG Novasoft Technologies Ltd. Madras High Court (Crl.R.C.No. 370 of 2014 order dated 02-09-2014. Original Petition No. 463 of 2012), (Indiankanoon.org., 2019). The victim was awarded a sum of INR Rs. 1.68 crores in damages as the company had not constituted a Complaint Committee in line with the Vishaka Judgement.

In order to make sure that the ICC embers can do their jobs responsibly, it is needed to train them about the law, the procedures and the skills needed to manage or address an issue as delicate as sexual harassment. The two most imperative skills for which ICC members must be trained are discussed below.

5.6.1. Handling Complaints Sensitively

The ICC members must be trained to look into all complaints and maters denoted to them sensitively and objectively. Probing incidents, asking questions, and trying to gain more information about reported incidents need a lot of skill and tact.

Bias and judgmental stances do a lot of damage and can deteriorate the protective social fabric of the organization. Facts should be amassed without taking sides, and in such situations, empathy is the key.

5.6.2. Handling Malicious Complaints

The flip side to strict policy implementation to deal with acts of "Sexual Harassment" is that it also entices malicious complaints. Such complaints are filed with a mala fide determination to discredit and harm a person, even though no such act has happened.

Malicious complaints with respect to the "Sexual Harassment" augments post appraisals or performance assessments (E and Y Report, 2015). Ensuring that everyone is aware of what "Sexual Harassment" is and what would happen if complaints are found malicious, could lessen the frequencies of false complaints.

5.7. WHEN SHOULD SUCH TRAINING PROGRAMS BE CONDUCTED? (FIGURE 5.3)

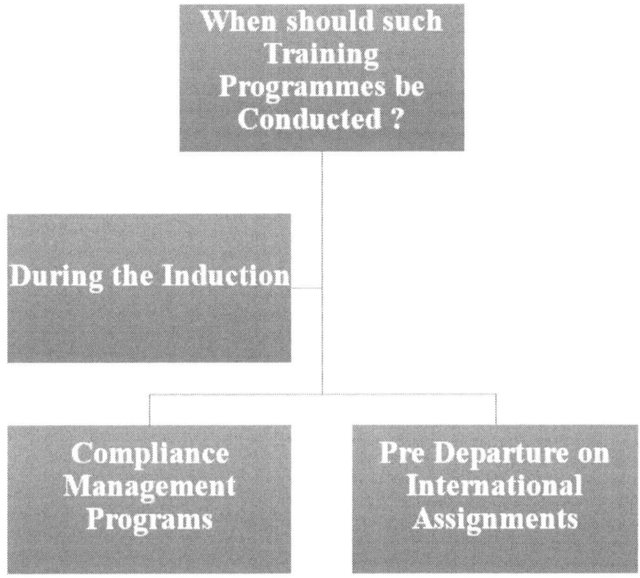

Figure 5.3. When should such training programs be conducted?

5.7.1. During the Induction

The induction program is the perfect time to teach the new hires about all the policies of the organization. The socialization of the employee should start with not just the mission and vision statements but also the values of the company. This is the perfect time for the employees to be well-versed about the company's stance towards sexual harassment.

It is the both the responsibility and accountability of the HR department and the organization to drive home the view that "Sexual Harassment" is a serious offence. The company policy with respect to "Sexual Harassment" should be explained clearly to employees, making them aware of what "Sexual Harassment" is, what are the effects of such actions, how to face such situations, who to complain to and so on.

5.7.2. Compliance Management Programs

Compliance management generally refers to the manner in which an organization pursues to educate and enforce on its employees the several internal policies/regulations, in addition to the government rules and regulations that the employee and the organization has and is obliged to follow.

Research has revealed that employees who receive compliance training are more productive, have lower turnover rates and higher retention rate, are more efficient and effective, and need less supervision. Majority of the employees know what are the do's and don'ts at the workplace, but all of them are not aware of what sort of acts of omission or commission would be regarded as improper and more imperatively, illegal. There are many minute and subtle issues that employees may not comprehend but which may violate company policy.

Making it obligatory for all employees to attend compliance management programs would help in making sure that employees have no misunderstanding of company's norms. When employees are fully aware about their compliance responsibilities, the result is an ethical workplace where employees develop a productive and respectful relationship.

5.7.3. Pre-Departure on International Assignments

Training an employee before he takes on an expatriate assignment should be intended at enhancing the employees understanding about the host country, the society he would live in, the values, the culture, and most significantly the dos and don'ts. Conducting such training before he leaves would assist in a better cross-cultural experience and helps in decline in misunderstandings.

5.8. HOW TO ENSURE THAT THE COMPANY'S "ANTI-SEXUAL HARASSMENT" TRAINING IS EFFECTIVE?

Ideally anti-sexual harassment training programs should commence immediately from the on boarding process. The company should make it crystal clear that acts of bullying intimidation or any other form of sexual harassment is a grave offence.

During the induction program, the company must have a complete introduction to the code of conduct of all employees, the actions that could constitute harassment as well as the dos and don'ts at work, even outside the physical premises of the organization.

The usage of more participative methods such as role plays, case studies, videos for the training would be more effectual to help employees getting aware about the company's stance on sexual harassment. Training should be steered across all levels, so that there is cognizance as well as a caution that any sort of behavior which even borders on sexual harassment will not be allowed.

Irrespective of how effective the induction training is, periodical campaigns, awareness through emails, posters must be an ongoing process, so that there is a reinforcement of learning:

- The compliance management program has to be effectively communicated. Stories/incidences that have happened must be used. It is one of the best ways to fetch employees' attention. The program has to be conveyed in simple language without using too much legal terminology or technical jargon.
- It is also important to note that learning has to be reinforced at periodic intervals. Change will be slow and cannot be attained overnight. Ideally employers must communicate evidently, steadily, and firmly what sort of behaviors are acceptable and what sort of behaviors, gestures, language, etc., are inadequate for the workplace.
- There should be proper use of pictures and images in order to make the training program more effective. Posters, circulars, and pictures in mails may make the understanding of delicate yet significant issues much easier. The training program can be supplemented with hand-outs of slides.
- A blend of offline and online training may be used to make the learning more effective and efficient.

5.9. HOW TO REPORT AN ALLEGATION OF SEXUAL HARASSMENT, HARASSMENT, DISCRIMINATION, AND/OR RETALIATION?

Any employee who witnesses, is subjected to, or becomes aware of harassment, sexual harassment, and/or discrimination should immediately report the incident. One who experienced such an incident can report it to their supervisor, agency ethics officer, the Illinois Department of Human Rights (IDHR), and/or the Office of Executive Inspector General (OEIG) (Figure 5.4).

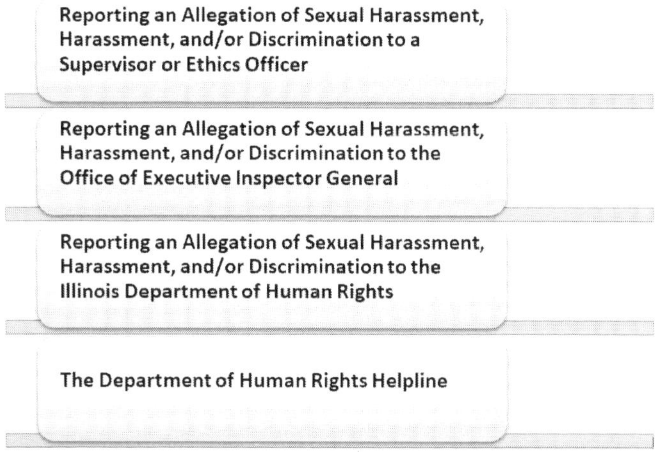

Figure 5.4. Bully, harassment, discrimination in the workplace.

In addition, if any employee experiences retaliation after reporting discrimination or harassment, that conduct can be conveyed to their supervisor, the OEIG, ethics officer, and the IDHR in the similar manner that harassment, sexual harassment, and discrimination are reported.

Occasionally, it is challenging to know whether the conduct that makes oneself feel uncomfortable is harassment, sexual harassment, or discrimination in violation of a law or policy. When in doubt, employees are persuaded to report inadequate conduct so that the employer can address the issue.

While majority of the training program focuses on the legal definitions of harassment, sexual harassment, and discrimination, the concerned company's policies may discuss additional conduct that is prohibited. It is imperative to know and recognize a company's policies and if one is unsure if something is inadequate to report the conduct so that it can be properly addressed.

5.9.1. Reporting an Allegation of Sexual Harassment, Harassment, and/or Discrimination to a Supervisor or Ethics Officer

One can report an allegation of harassment, sexual harassment, and/or discrimination to a supervisor. Supervisors have comprehensive understanding about the internal practices of their company, and will be in a position to effect transition and to assist the victim in navigating the agency's internal complaint process.

Although supervisors may obtain assistance from or report the allegation to the agency ethics officer, they should share only the information that is required by law or in order to effect crucial management action to address one's allegation.

One can also report an allegation of harassment, sexual harassment, and/or discrimination to their ethics officer. Ethics officer of the concerned person is available to discuss any issues about ethics violations that one may have.

Ethics officers can assist in interpreting the Ethics Act for the person as well as their agency policies that forbid harassment, sexual harassment, and discrimination. Ethics officers will be well-informed about the reporting process for the IDHR and OEIG, and can assist oneself in making a report to these entities or to their supervisor or another manager.

In addition, if an allegation of harassment, sexual harassment, and/or discrimination comprises supervisor, or if a person is uncomfortable with your supervisor or are concerned that the allegation may not be handled by the supervisor properly, in that case one can report the allegation directly to their ethics officer, IDHR, and/or the OEIG.

5.9.2. Reporting an Allegation of Sexual Harassment, Harassment, and/or Discrimination to the Office of Executive Inspector General (OEIG)

It is worth noticing that OEIG is an independent executive branch State agency that works to ensure accountability in State government.

The OEIG's jurisdiction comprises executive branch agencies, officers, and employees (other than those under the Attorney General, Secretary of State, Treasurer or Comptroller), the four regional transit boards, the State public universities, and about 300 commissions and boards, plus vendors doing business with those entities and agencies.

The OEIG does not exemplify any party or agency in an investigation nor does it scrutinize on behalf of any agency or individual. The solo objective of the OEIG is to investigate allegations of misconduct and to publish reports of its findings to the affected officials and agencies.

The OEIG investigates, when adequate, alleged violations of rule, law or regulation committed by any employee of, or those doing business with, an entity under its jurisdiction. For instance, the OEIG investigates allegations of fraud, waste, corruption, or abuse of authority.

The OEIG investigates violations of the Ethics Act that comprises a prohibition on sexual harassment. A complaint may be filed with the OEIG in writing, ideally on an OEIG complaint form, or orally. A complaint may be filed with the OEIG by:

- Completing a form online at http://www.inspectorgeneral.illinois.gov;
- Calling the toll-free hotline number of OEIG's at (866) 814–1113;
- Mailing a full complaint form to: OEIG for the Agencies of the Illinois Governor, 69 West Washington Street, Attention Complaint Division, Suite 3400, Chicago, Illinois 60602;
- Faxing a completed complaint form to (312) 814–5479;
- Contacting the OEIG by telecommunications device for the disabled (TTY) at (888) 261–2734; or
- Scheduling an appointment with its Chicago or Springfield locations.

The OEIG may also accept complaints that are filed incognito. Anyone filing a complaint should provide enough detail about the allegation so that comprehensive investigation can be initiated.

Pursuant to the Ethics Act, "the identity of any individual conveying information or reporting any alleged or possible misconduct to an Executive Inspector General or the Executive Ethics Commission shall be kept confidential and may not be disclosed without the individual's consent, unless the individual consents to disclosure of her or his name or disclosure of the identity of the individual is otherwise required by law."

5.9.3. Reporting an Allegation of Sexual Harassment, Harassment, and/or Discrimination to the Illinois Department of Human Rights (IDHR)

The IDHR is basically a state agency that oversees the Human Rights Act. Individuals can report an allegation of harassment, sexual harassment, and/or discrimination to the IDHR by filing a charge within 300 days of the alleged incident.

The first and foremost step in filing a charge is to submit information in person or in writing by fax or mail with the help of a Complainant Information Sheet that is available on the IDHR website. It needs comprehensive information, including contact information, the most recent date of the alleged conduct, and employer information. A person filing a charge may also offer witness information and copies of pertinent documents. The IDHR website is www.illinois.gov/dhr. It offers extra information about harassment and discrimination, filing a charge, the complete procedure for investigating and resolving an allegation, and other FAQs.

5.9.4. The Department of Human Rights Helpline

The IDHR operates a helpline for reporting sexual harassment and discrimination. The helpline number is 1-877-236-7703. In addition to this, there is also a website for reporting: https://www2.illinois.gov/sites/sexualharassment/Pages/default.aspx.

Through the helpline:

- individuals can receive help along with the essential related resources, including counseling services;
- individuals can receive support with filing sexual harassment as well as discrimination complaints with the IDHR or other agencies;
- individuals may anonymously report sexual harassment as well as discrimination in both private-sector and State employment;
- For individuals who are subject to the Ethics Act, the IDHR will report the allegations to the OEIG for further investigation if the person formulating the report gives the IDHR permission.

All communication offered to the IDHR through the helpline, composed by the Internet, will be confidential and exempted from disclosure under the Freedom of Information Act.

5.10. INFORMATION ABOUT RETALIATION

Retaliation against individuals who report harassment, sexual harassment, and/or discrimination, or who participate in investigations and other proceedings concerning those matters, is strictly prohibited by the human rights act, ethics act, and the Illinois Whistle-Blower Act (Figure 5.5).

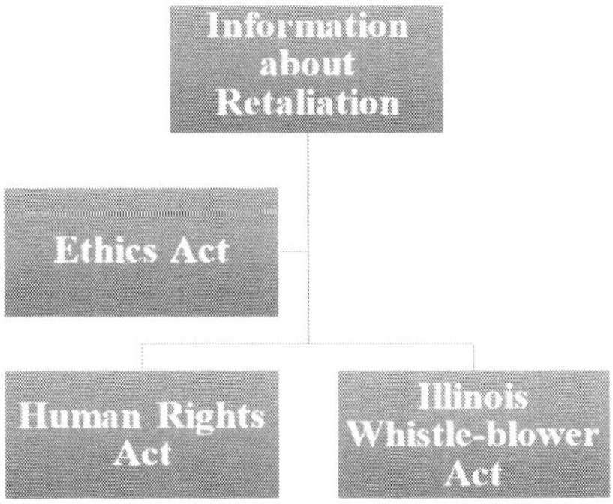

Figure 5.5. Information about retaliation.

5.10.1. Ethics Act

An officer, State employee, member, or State agency shall not take any retaliatory action against a state employee because the state employee:

- Discloses or warns to disclose to a supervisor or to a public body a policy, activity, or practice of any officer, State agency, member, or other State employee that the State employee rationally believes is in violation of a rule, law, or regulation.
- Provides information to or testifies before any public body leading an investigation, inquiry, or hearing into any violation of a rule, law, or regulation by any member, officer, State agency, or other State employee.
- Participates or Assists in a proceeding to enforce the Ethics Act provisions.

Retaliatory action means reprimand, suspension, discharge, demotion, denial of transfer or promotion, or change in the terms or conditions of employment of an employee that arises in retaliation for an employee's participation in the protected activities discussed above.

If retaliatory action arises, the OEIG can examine the matter and endorse discipline. An employee can also bring a lawsuit pursuant to the Ethics Act. Anyone who deliberately defies this prohibition on retaliation is guilty of a misdemeanor and is subject to discharge or discipline.

5.10.2. Human Rights Act

It is a civil rights violation to react against a person who opposes that which they rationally and in good faith consider to be sexual harassment or unlawful discrimination. 775 ILCS 5/6-101(A). For instance, it is unlawful for someone to retaliate against a person who filed a complaint, participated in an investigation or enquiry, or testified regarding a matter under the Human Rights Act.

5.10.3. Illinois Whistle-Blower Act

An employer may not retaliate against an employee "for disclosing information to a government or law enforcement agency, where the employee has reasonable cause to believe that the information discloses a violation of a State or federal law, rule, or regulation." 740 ILCS 174/15(b).

Furthermore, an employer shall not retaliate against an employee for declining to participate in an activity that would result in a violation of a federal or State law, rule, or regulation. If an employer reacts against an employee in violation of the Illinois Whistle-blower Act, and the employee accomplishes in a civil suit, the employee may get relief essential to make the employee whole, embracing reinstatement into their position, and back pay with interest, and reimbursement for damages.

5.11. THE TROUBLE WITH HARASSMENT TRAINING

The harassment training that focuses on forbidden behaviors, does it decrease the rate of harassment? Apparently not. When organizations and firms establish this sort of training, it has been observed that women in management lose ground. In order to isolate the impacts of these sorts of programs, advanced statistical techniques have been used in order to account for other alterations in an organization, its industry, and its state that might be impacting the numbers of women in management.

It has been seen that when organizations or firms institute forbidden-behavior training programs, the representation of white women in management drops by more than 5% over the following few years. Asian American, African American, and Latina women do not tend to lose ground after these types of harassment training is founded-but they do not gain it either. White women make up near about 33% of all women in management and half of all women in the workforce, in such a way that as a group they bear most of the training backlash.

5.11.1. Research Shows That Harassment Training Makes Men More Likely to Blame the Victims

Why would training designed to educate employees about the harassment that institutes a backlash? That seems counterintuitive. The issue is with how the training is presented. Generally, it is compulsory, which sends the message that men have to be forced to pay attention to the problem. And its emphases on the forbidden behaviors, the essentials, which indicates that the men do not know where the line is. The message is that men need fixing.

Start any training by telling a bunch of people that they are the issue, and probably, they will get defensive. Once that happens, they are much less likely to want to be a part of the solution; as an alternative, the men will resist. That is what happens with harassment training: according to the numerous researches that shows that it actually makes men that are more likely to blame the victims and to think that women who files the complaint against harassment are making it up or overreacting.

No surprise, then, that according to a study which is carried by the Pew Research Center in 2018, more than 30% of men said that wrong acquisitions of sexual harassment are "a major issue." And no surprise that 58% of women who had been harassed said that not being believed is a major problem.

This dynamic plays out in anticipated ways-out of which, one is that men put on the defensive, make gags or fun about the training sessions and about harassment as well. The phenomenon is so common that the writers of TV show, known as The Office focused an entire episode to it. At one point Pam, who plays the character of a receptionist, wearily tells the camera, "Usually, the day we talk about sexual harassment is the day everyone harasses me as a joke."

What about men who are prone to harass? The reason is that training is very essential to reach those men. Does training help those men, at least? No. It has been seen that the men who tend to harass women before training actually become more accepting of these types of behavior after the training.

However, what do organizations or firms commonly do when they find out that the men are responsible in a grievance process? Sentence them to more training. Six states, including California and New York, now necessitate all employers to provide harassment training to all employees or workforces.

5.11.2. Training Alternatives

If the distinctive harassment training leads to the loss of female management executives and makes the bad guys a little worse, then probably it is time to start thinking about the types of training that are way more effective. There are two types of training that potentially overcome this issue and are mentioned below.

5.11.3. Bystander-Intervention Training

Bystander-intervention training is the most effective option to the issue. Sharyn Potter and her team at the University of New Hampshire's Prevention Innovation Research Center have conducted an interesting experiment within the premises of college and military bases, where the cases of harassment and assault are extensive. Few years ago, Sharyn Potter and her team piloted a college bystander-intervention program that has since been used on more than 300 campuses. Then it was adapted for the U.S. Army in 2011.

In their programs, Potter, and her team start with the hypothesis that the trainees are associates working to find the solution to the issues that are related to harassment and assault instead of potential perps. Everybody's job is to find out the misbehavior in the college. Basically, it is the "If you see something, say (or do) something" approach. Properly trained bystanders interrupt the sexual joke.

They call out the catcallers. They distract the drunk pair who have just met but are set to leave the party together. The approach surprisingly turned out very efficient. Scholars and soldiers who have taken part in bystander training constantly reported that it has helped them in order to know what to do when they see signs of a problem. Importantly, even after the months of the training, trainees are considerably more likely as compared to the others report having intervened in real-life scenarios.

Word is getting out about the merits of bystander training. Potter now leads a nonprofit organization that develops programs for organizations of all sorts. The U.S. Air Force has developed its own. When the city of New York mandated in 2018 that all employers provide harassment training, it also mandated them to cover bystander intervention and offered a model online program which is free of cost to the employers.

Inopportunely, the entire program lasts for only 45 minutes or so and covers five topics, which is mainly consisting of forbidden behaviors. That is a far cry from what studies have found to be efficient for the scholars who are studying in college as well as the military personnel: few hours of live training that focuses on bystander intervention.

5.11.4. Manager Training

In manager training programs, the training is delivered exclusively to the management executives, which is also found quite efficient. It has been seen that organizations or firms that implemented the distinct manager-training programs saw gains in the percentage of women in their managerial ranks in considerable amounts, with white women rising by more than 6%, African American and Asian American women by 5%, and Latinas by 2%.

Manager training work out and the reason behind this is that, it depicts the harassment as a challenge that all management executives must deal with. Hence, it looks a lot like bystander training. Participants, men, and women alike, are motivated to imagine what they might see other people doing wrong; the main emphasis is intentionally not on what they themselves might do wrong. Trainers give recommendations to the participants on how to distinguish early signs of harassment and how to face it or cope-up with it, swiftly, and efficiently in order to stop the escalation.

It has been seen that men pay attention through the course of manager training. Why? In part, and the reason behind this is that the men feel they are being given new tools that will help them solve the issues they have not known how to cope-up with in the past times and in part because they are assumed to be potential heroes instead of being villains. Everybody is in it together, learning how to identify and curb dubious behaviors in such a way that it will enhance the overall work environment.

5.12. THE TROUBLE WITH GRIEVANCE PROCEDURES

The evidence on forbidden behavior training is crystal clear: It is worth noticing that it is not helping us much to solve the problem of workplace sexual harassment. But what about legalistic grievance procedures?

It is generally seen that every Fortune 500 company has a grievance procedure. These procedures were first cooked up by lawyers to intercept victims who were planning to sue, and then were adapted to safeguard companies against suits by the accused.

But they have not helped in making the situation better for women. After the companies in our study applied them, in fact, the total number of women working in management deteriorated. The biggest failures occurred in companies with few female managers. It is due to the fact that women are more likely than men to believe reports of harassment. When there are limited female managers to obtain reports, victims who complain are occasionally given the third degree that results in prompting them to quit. At companies having the fewest female managers to begin with (those in the lowest quartile), the introduction of harassment grievance procedures resulted in considerable declines, over several years, of 14% among African American, 10% among Latina, and 10% among Asian American female managers.

The negative effects were meagre at companies having more women in managerial roles, and they vanished in organizations with the most. Numbers of white women in management were not affected by grievance procedures.

Then it is important to ask why did women of color suffer most? Studies show that they are drastically more likely than white women to be harassed at work. As these women bear the brunt of harassment, as a group they file the most complaints—and, naturally, hurt the most when grievance procedures backfire.

But it is equally imperative to ask why do those procedures backfire? The answer, according to a variety of studies, is revenge against victims who complain. One survey of federal workers found that 66% of women who had reported their harassers were consequently assaulted, demoted, taunted, or even fired by their harassers or friends of their harassers.

It is generally seen that this kind of retaliation has long-term effects. Women who file harassment complaints end up, on average, in inferior jobs and poorer mental and physical health than do women who keep quiet. And retaliation may be the only thing many victims get after filing a grievance, as the majority of the procedures safeguard the accused better than they protect victims.

Part of the problem is that privacy rules are unenforceable and thus cannot avert retribution. Both the accused and their accusers are told that the complaint is trustworthy as the accused is innocent until proven guilty. Those accused generally believe they are free to tell their friends, and managers who hear complaints may also tell others, looking for either support or corroboration for the accused. No matter how word gets out, friends of the accused may retaliate.

After an Ohio waitress criticized harassment, the female manager she told disclosed her complaint to co-workers, who subjected the waitress to nonstop jokes. Another part of the problem is evidentiary rules. Majority of the companies use the "beyond a reasonable doubt" standard to decide guilt, not the lower "preponderance of evidence" standard that the courts take into use for harassment claims.

That makes it almost unbearable to prove guilt without a confession or a witness. Even in case the accused is found guilty, confidentiality normally applies to the ruling, and therefore word does not get out that, say, women should steer clear of Jerry.

Women who reported their harassers were subsequently assaulted, demoted, or fired. Yet another is an unwillingness to punish perpetrators. Companies occasionally likes to transfer victims to other locations or departments, but they almost never actually fire or transfer the accused, as they worry that the accused will sue. Instead, they typically command more training.

It is generally seen that several companies even keep verdicts secret from accusers that could even result in the perverse outcome: A victim who has "won" her case sees her harasser roaming the halls, and considering that this means she has lost it, she becomes frustrated or dispirited or angry and decides to leave her job.

But victims who have to experience retaliation after complaining often quit well before the process is complete. That is what happened in September 2019, after Broti Gupta, a writer for the CBS sitcom Carol's Second Act, complained of intimate touching by an executive producer with the network, which had just reviewed its complaint system to advance the treatment of accusers.

HR went legalistic and permitted new rules to keep writers and producers apart. Gupta quit, saying she had been cut out of the creative process in retaliation. Margee Magee, a writer who took her side, told the New York Times, "All we required was for him to watch like a 45-minute harassment video. None of this had to happen."

The evidence is clear-cut: Our present grievance system puts victims at a distinct difficulty, through unenforceable secrecy rules, a high evidentiary bar, and penalties that leave harassers in place. Furthermore, everybody knows that the system is rigged. Because of this reason, HR officers generally counsel victims against filing grievances—and why studies display that only about one in 10 victims makes a formal complaint. The messages you can read in posts at #WhyIDidntReport say it all: They won't believe me. They'll put me through a sham hearing. The guy will get off. He'll try to get back at me. His buddies will think I did something to deserve it. Accusers have only two real options: report harassment and suffer the consequences, or don't report it.

5.13. CONCLUSION

At the end, it is concluded that anti sexual harassment training is now one of the most important things that every company should take care of. In the past few years, there has been increase in incidence for sexual harassment. Such behavior should not be tolerated in the organization as it results in causing lower productivity, lower retention rate as well as other financial burden. Investing in the anti-sexual harassment training is worth considering as it helps company saving a lot in terms of both money and reputation. In addition, there should be adequate procedures for reporting such incidents as inefficiency of these could result in serious consequences for both the victim and company. Such incidents should be reported and adequate actions should be taken so that it deters others from being involved in such type of behavior. Every employee should have made aware about different types of sexual harassment so that they can report the same if they face any. Training must be provided to the new employees as they could be potentially exploited due to lack of awareness.

REFERENCES

1. (2010). Guide on Prevention of Sexual Harassment in the Workplace. [eBook] Beijing Zhongze Women's Legal Consultation and Service Center-Women Watch China. Available at: https://www.ilo.org/wcmsp5/groups/public/---asia/---ro-bangkok/---ilo-beijing/documents/publication/wcms_157626.pdf (accessed on 17 August 2021).
2. (2015). Sexual Harassment Prevention Made Simple Facilitator's Guide. [eBook] TrainingABC. Available at: https://www.uttyler.edu/human-resources/files/shms_facilitator.pdf (accessed on 17 August 2021).
3. (2019). Model Sexual Harassment Prevention Training October 2019 Edition. [eBook] Available at: https://www.ny.gov/sites/default/files/atoms/files/SexualHarassmentPreventionModelTraining.pdf (accessed on 17 August 2021).
4. (2020). 2020 Harassment and Discrimination Prevention Training. [eBook] Available at: https://equity.siu.edu/_common/documents/training/2020sexualharassment.pdf (accessed on 17 August 2021).
5. Arora, K., (2020). Anti-Sexual Harassment Training: A Must for Indian Companies. [Online] Ungender | Empaneled by GoI. Available at: https://www.ungender.in/why-companies-need-anti-sexual-harassment-training/ (accessed on 17 August 2021).
6. Bala, S., (2021). Training Module on Prevention of Sexual Harassment of women at Workplace. [eBook] Available at: https://vvgnli.gov.in/sites/default/files/TRANING%20MODULE%20ON%20SEXUAL%20HARASSMENT%20OF%20WOMEN%20AT%20WORKPLACE.pdf (accessed on 17 August 2021).
7. Harvard Business Review, (2020). Why Sexual Harassment Programs Backfire. [Online] Available at: https://hbr.org/2020/05/why-sexual-harassment-programs-backfire (accessed on 17 August 2021).
8. Shivakumar, K., (2020). Prevention of "Sexual Harassment" at the Workplace-can Training Help? [Online] www.researchgate.net. Available at: https://www.researchgate.net/publication/339507834_Prevention_of_Sexual_Harassment_at_the_Workplace-Can_Training_Help (accessed on 17 August 2021).

9. Talentpro India, (2021). Importance and Benefits of Prevention of Sexual Harassment Training (POSH) for Your Employees | Talentpro India. [Online] Available at: https://www.talentproindia.com/2021/04/27/importance-and-benefits-of-prevention-of-sexual-harassment-training-for-your-employees-posh/ (accessed on 17 August 2021)

Chapter 6

Policy Creation and Communication

CONTENTS

In this chapter the anti-harassment policy creation and communication to employees in a corporate organization has been discussed in detail. The anti-harassment policy and complaints have also been discussed in this chapter.

The globalization and creation of corporate anti-harassment policies in multinational corporations (MNCs) has also been discussed in detail. The directions to write a code of conduct for employees in the workplace has been discussed in detail.

The effective communication of anti-harassment policies to employees has also been discussed in this chapter.

6.1. INTRODUCTION

In a worldwide market, major businesses must be able to adapt to changes in their operating environment. When rules of behavior, which are often believed to be stable, come into contact with cultural norms that differ from one another in the international workplace, difficulties occur. Codes of conduct are composed of policies that workers are required to follow. One part of these regulations that has the potential to be problematic is the policy pertaining to sexual harassment.

When it comes to sexual harassment regulations, there needs to be an ethical norm established between the individual employee and the organization. In terms of worldwide tolerance for sexual harassment, this ethical criterion should not serve as the overriding baseline. Businesses face a number of ethical and financial challenges as a result of sexual harassment in a worldwide economy.

As a result, corporations have gone to considerable efforts to convey codes of conduct that regulate behavior to all of their employees. In terms of productivity and legal difficulties, it is predicted that sexual harassment would become increasingly costly to global enterprises in the next decades. It is protected by Title VII of the Civil Rights Act, which was modified by Congress in 1991 to create a mechanism for victims to seek compensatory damages and back pay (Roberts, B. S., and Mann, R. A.).

According to Stanko and Schneider (1999), 90% of Fortune 500 firms have received sexual harassment accusations, with claim resolution expenses averaging $200,000 on average (Keyton, Ferguson, and Rhodes, 2001).

It was recently determined that businesses can be held responsible for up to 500,000 dollars in damages for sexual harassment, even if the company's senior officials were unaware of any harassing activity on their property (All Business Website, 2006).

Because of the growing financial cost associated with sexual harassment litigation, it appears that businesses have determined that it is important to create rules within their codes of conduct and ethics that are more comprehensive in nature. This would imply that organizations are becoming more proactive in tackling the issue of harassment inside their organizations, therefore reducing the cost burden associated with lawsuits and other legal proceedings.

Because of the widespread use of legal definitions of sexual harassment since the 1970s in Western societies, sexual harassment has been connected with multi-million dollars lawsuits that have altered public attitudes of appropriate workplace speech.

As demonstrated by the over 15,000 accusations of sexual harassment filed and handled with the United States (U.S.) government in the year 2000, sexual harassment has become an increasingly prevalent issue in American workplaces (Keyton, Ferguson, and Rhodes, 2001). According to Mulligan and Foy (2003) 15,475 sexual harassment complaints were filed in 2001, and 14,396 charges were filed in 2002, respectively.

The U.S. is not the only industrialized country to be confronted with the issue of sexual harassment and assault. A survey conducted by Bridge (1997) found that 30% of Australia's 14,000 (4,200) female naval personnel and civilian workers had experienced harassment (Mackay, 2001).

Around 40% of working women in Japan experienced sexual harassment, which might include sexual jokes, comments about physical appearance or marital status, unwelcome physical contact, obscene telephone calls and letters, requests for sex from male colleagues in positions of authority, or sexual attacks from male colleagues (Mackay, 2001; Human Rights Report, 1996; National Personnel Authority Survey, 1996).

Sexual harassment has evolved into a worldwide issue that affects people all over the world. It is critical that sexual harassment regulations for a multinational marketplace are conveyed to employees in a way that is sensitive to cultural differences (Figure 6.1).

Figure 6.1. Brainstorming of human resources over policy creation and communication.

Source: Image by Pxhere.

6.2. ANTI-HARASSMENT POLICY AND COMPLAINTS

When it comes to creating and maintaining a work environment where individuals are treated with dignity, decency, and respect, companies try to do so. Mutual trust, as well as a lack of intimidation, tyranny, and exploitation, should define the workplace environment of the firm in which it operates.

The organization will not accept any form of unlawful discrimination or harassment, regardless of the source. The organization will endeavor to prevent, rectify, and penalize behavior that is in violation of this policy through the enforcement of this policy and the education of workers.

This policy applies to all workers, regardless of their position, and all employees are required to follow it and to take reasonable steps to ensure that prohibited conduct does not occur. Any employee who breaches this policy will be subjected to the appropriate disciplinary action under the law. A verbal or written reprimand, suspension, or termination of work may be appropriate depending on the gravity of the violation committed.

Infringing on this policy and subjecting themselves to disciplinary action are managers and supervisors who intentionally enable or tolerate discrimination, harassment, or retaliation, including failing to immediately report such misbehavior to human resources (HRs).

6.2.1. Prohibited Conduct Under This Policy

Compliance with all relevant anti-discrimination and harassment laws and regulations on a federal, state, and local level is required by organization, which implements this policy in accordance with the definitions and standards set out in further sections.

6.2.2. Discrimination

It is a violation, wholly or partially, of the organization policy to discriminate against employees, benefits, and privileges; create conditions of discrimination on employment; or use discriminatory evaluative standards in employment where the race, color, national origin, age, religion, status of disability, sex or sexual orientation are the basis for this discriminatory treatment.

In addition, a number of federal, state, and municipal laws, including Title VII of the Civil Rights Act of 1964, the Age Discrimination Act of 1967, and the Americans with Disabilities Act of 1990, may make it illegal to discriminate on the basis of race, religion, or national origin. The purpose of this policy is to ensure that it complies with the anti-discrimination legislation that have been enacted.

Individuals found to be discriminating against others in violation of this policy will face disciplinary action, which may include termination.

6.2.3. Harassment

The organization forbids harassment of any type, including sexual harassment, and will take appropriate and quick action in response to complaints or knowledge of violations of this policy. The organization is committed to protecting its employees from all forms of harassment. To be considered harassing for the purposes of this policy, any verbal or physical behavior that is intended to intimidate, threaten, or force an employee, coworker, or any other person working for or on behalf of the organization is prohibited.

When assessing whether or not there has been a breach of this policy, the following instances of harassment are meant to serve as suggestions only and are not intended to be exhaustive:

- It includes remarks that are derogatory or unwelcome in nature and that are directed at a person's national origin or race or color or religion or age or sexual orientation or pregnancy or other protected status, as well as insults and slurs directed at that person's appearance or disability or gender identity or expression or marital status or other protected status.

- In addition to verbal harassment, nonverbal harassment includes the distribution, display, or discussion of any written or graphic material that disparages, insults, belittles, or otherwise expresses hostility, aversion, or disrespect toward an individual or group on the basis of their national origin or race or color or religion or age or gender or sexual orientation or pregnancy or their appearance or disability or sexual identity or marital status or any other protected status.

6.2.4. Sexual Harassment

The practice of sexual harassment is forbidden under the organization anti-harassment policy, which is in accordance with Title VII of the Civil Rights Act of 1964. According to the Equal Employment Opportunity Commission (EEOC), sexual harassment is defined as unwelcome sexual advances, requests for sexual favors, and other verbal or physical conduct of a sexual nature when submission to or rejection of such conduct is used as the basis for employment decisions or when such conduct has the purpose or effect of creating an intimidating, hostile, or harassing work environment.

Sexual harassment occurs when an employer makes unwelcome and uninvited sexual approaches, demands for sexual favors, or other verbal or physical activity of a sexual character a condition of employment, whether expressly or implicitly.

- Is utilized to make a choice on whether or not to hire someone;
- Creates an intimidating, hostile, or otherwise unpleasant work environment by interfering with an employee's ability to execute their job duties in an unreasonable manner.

Sexual harassment can manifest itself in a variety of ways. When assessing whether or not there has been a violation of this policy, the following instances of sexual harassment are meant to serve as suggestions only and are not intended to be exhaustive:

- The term verbal sexual harassment includes innuendos, suggestive comments, sexually explicit jokes, sexual propositions, lewd remarks, and threats; requests for any type of sexual favor this includes repeated, unwelcome requests for dates; and verbal abuse or kidding that is directed at or oriented toward a prohibited form of harassment, including that which is sexual in nature and unwelcome.

- The distribution, display, or discussion of any written or graphic material, including calendars, posters, and cartoons, that is sexually suggestive or shows hostility toward an individual or group because of sex; suggestive or insulting sounds; leering; staring; whistling; obscene gestures; content in letters, notes, facsimiles, e-mails, photos, text messages, or any other written or graphic material; and any written or graphic material that is sexually suggestive or
- In addition to undesired and unwanted physical contact, such as touching, tickling, pinching, patting, and brushing up against, embracing, and cornering, kissing, and fondling, and forced sexual intercourse or assault, physical sexual harassment can involve threats of violence.

Interactions between workers that are courteous, mutually respectful, pleasant, and noncoercive, and that are suitable in the workplace and acceptable to and welcomed by both parties are not considered harassment, including sexual harassment.

6.2.5. Consensual Romantic or Sexual Relationships

In order to avoid compromising conflicts of interest or the appearance of compromising conflicts of interest, the organization strongly discourages romantic or sexual relationships between managers or other supervisory employees and employees who report directly or indirectly to those managers or other supervisory employees.

In addition, such a connection may give rise to the belief by others that there is favoritism or prejudice in employment decisions impacting the staff employee who is involved in the relationship. More importantly, due to the unequal power dynamics that exist in such partnerships, any permission provided by the staff member is questionable and may be seen by others, or even by the staff member themselves, as having been obtained by force or intimidation in the first place.

When there are indications of prejudice, favoritism, intimidation, coercion, or exploitation, the climate generated by these factors weakens the spirit of trust and mutual respect that is vital to a productive workplace environment. If such a connection exists, the parties should be informed that one or both of them may be transferred to a different department or that other actions may be taken against them. A consensual sexual or romantic relationship between any organization employee and another employee who reports directly or indirectly to that employee, or if one of the parties is in a supervisory capacity in the same department in which the other party works, the parties must notify the organization HRs director or other appropriate corporate officer.

The required reporting of quid pro quo harassment has been implemented by organization due to the possibility of quid pro quo harassment. There are certain exceptions, such as workers who do not work in the same department or parties in which neither party supervises or has other control over their respective counterparts' duties and obligations.

Once the organization is aware of the relationship, the company will consult with HRs to assess the situation in light of all the facts including the reporting relationship between the parties, the effect on co-workers, the job titles of the parties, and so on and will determine whether one or both of the parties should be transferred to another position or department.

The parties may select who will apply for a new post if it is decided that one of them must be relocated and there are positions in other departments available for both of them. If the parties are unable to reach an agreement amicably, or if the party is not selected for the post for which he or she applied, the HRs director and senior management will determine which party will be relocated.

Ultimately, the decision will be made based on whatever option will cause the least amount of disruption to the company as a whole. If neither partner can find another employment, the parties will be offered the option of dissolving their relationship or resigning from their positions.

6.2.6. Retaliation

It is prohibited to impose any type of hardship, loss, benefit, or penalty on an employee in response to the following actions:

- Filing or reacting to a legitimate complaint of discrimination or harassment;
- Appearing as a witness in an inquiry into a complaint is another option;
- Acting as an investigator in the case of a complaint.

The filing of a legitimate complaint will not be utilized against the employee and will not have any negative consequences for the individual's work situation. Filing unfounded or malicious complaints, on the other hand, is considered an abuse of this policy and will be addressed as such.

Any employee who is found to have violated this element of the policy may be subject to disciplinary action, which may include dismissal from the company altogether.

6.2.7. Confidentiality

All complaints and investigations are treated as secret to the greatest degree feasible, and information is only shared with those who have a legitimate need to know. After the inquiry is completed, the complainant's name is generally released to the parties involved.

The HRs manager is responsible for taking appropriate actions to ensure that the complainant is safeguarded from retribution both during and after the investigation. Unless otherwise specified, any information relating to a complaint or inquiry conducted under this policy shall be kept in secure files within the HRs department.

6.2.8. Complaint Procedure

In order to file a complaint of harassment, discrimination, or retaliation against [Company Name], the company has created the following procedure:

- To the greatest degree practically feasible, the firm will maintain the confidentiality of all parts of the procedure.
- If a complaint is filed as quickly as possible after an occurrence occurs, it is preferable that it be presented in writing.
- Employees who refuse to submit information in writing may be assisted by the HRs director in preparing a written statement, or the HR director may dictate a spoken complaint if an employee refuses to provide information in writing. The HRs director shall alert senior management and consult with the company's legal counsel upon receipt of a complaint or notification from a supervisor or manager that a breach of this policy may be taking place.
- In the third step, the HR director will launch an investigation to establish if there is a reasonable basis to believe that the claimed breach of this policy happened.

- The complainant and respondent will be separated if required, either by internal transfer or administrative leave, for the duration of the inquiry.
- In order to assess whether or not the claimed behavior took place, the HR director, in consultation with legal counsel or other management personnel, will interview the complainant, the respondent, and any witnesses during the inquiry process.
- After an investigation is completed, the HR director or other person in charge of the inquiry will present a written report to the firm detailing the results of the investigation. It will be the HR director's responsibility to evaluate whether or not a breach of this policy has occurred and to propose appropriate disciplinary action. The proper course of action will be determined by the following considerations:
  - The intensity, frequency, and pervasiveness of the behavior; and the duration of the conduct;
  - In the case of a previous complaint filed by the complainant;
  - Previous complaints lodged against the respondent;
  - The level of evidence's credibility like firsthand knowledge, credible corroboration.

Alternatively, if the inquiry is found to be inconclusive or if it is established that there has been no breach of policy but that potentially problematic behavior has occurred, the HRs director may propose appropriate preventative action:

- Upon completion of the inquiry, senior management will evaluate the report and any comments made by either the complainant or the responder, consult with the HR director and other management personnel as needed, and determine what action, if anything, will be taken.
- Once a final decision has been reached by senior management, the HR director will meet with both the complainant and the respondent individually to discuss the results of the inquiry and to notify them of the findings. If disciplinary action is to be taken, the respondent will be notified of the nature of the discipline as well as the manner in which it will be carried out by the organization.

6.2.9. Alternative Legal Remedies

Neither the complaint nor the responder is prohibited from seeking formal legal remedies or dispute resolution through local, state, or federal authorities or the courts if this policy is violated (Figure 6.2).

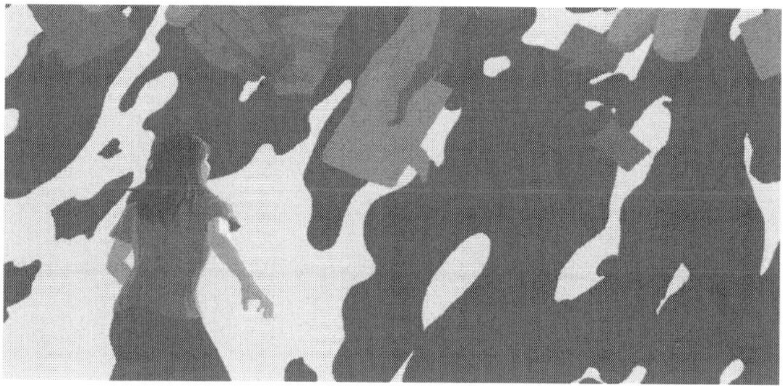

Figure 6.2. Harassment of employees in workplace.

Source: Image by MsMagazine.

6.3. GLOBALIZATION AND CORPORATE ANTI-HARASSMENT POLICY

A company that conducts business both inside and outside the borders of its nation of origin is referred to as a globalized corporation. The majority of globalization is occurring as a result of the expansion of firms in industrialized countries, notably American corporations, into new countries and markets. The process of corporate diversification happens when a company organization looks for opportunities to expand into markets outside of its home nation in order to conduct business on a global scale.

The employees and the company must negotiate culture on a variety of levels as part of the process of conducting business in a globalized economy. Interconnectedness is one aspect of globalization, while identification is another. Globalization is also a worldwide phenomenon, and it is not the result of Americanization.

The definition of globalization is extremely important for this study since globalization has an impact on the way companies establish codes of conduct for their employees. Globalization Has Many Faces The phrase globalization is interconnectivity refers to the way in which the globalization system stays dynamic and is able to keep firms connected in a globally competitive economy. In terms of interconnectedness, Friedman (1999) defines globalization as follows: It is the inexorable integration of markets, nation-states, and technologies in a way that is enabling individuals, corporations, and nation-states to reach around the world farther, faster, deeper, and cheaper than they ever have before, and in a way that is enabling the world to reach individuals, corporations, and nation-states farther, faster, deeper, and cheaper than they ever have before (Friedman, 1999).

Globalization has made it possible for companies to contact individuals more readily, and for individuals to reach corporations more easily. This capacity to communicate with one another from anywhere in the globe fosters a sense of belonging.

Reaching around the world in a more efficient, quicker, deeper, and more affordable manner has enabled firms to expand their operations to the most remote corners of the planet, resulting in the creation of the globalized marketplace.

Because of the linked nature of the system, individuals inside these organizations find it necessary to adapt to new cultural subtleties as they emerge. Globalization is an identifier that refers to the fact that individuals must make an effort to retain their own identities inside their different global organizations as a result of the system of globalization. In this view, globalization is a process through which individuals become more similar to persons in other companies.

Individuals struggle to define or restructure their own distinctive identities inside their separate companies; yet globalization pushes them to define or restructure their identities in order to suit the needs of the globalized enterprise.

According to Friedman (1999), people, and countries are challenged to strike a healthy balance between retaining one's sense of belonging and belonging to one's community while operating within the globalized system. Individuals may find themselves becoming more similar to their colleagues inside the business who are located in different nations as a result of this.

The third aspect of globalization may be seen in the very definition of the term globalization. In other words, the word itself contains the essence of what defines globalization as a phenomenon. Organizations and individuals interact as a result of globalization, which occurs through a variety of technical, informational, and financial ways. The notion of being global refers to the interaction of persons from various cultural backgrounds as well as the process of bringing them together in a global marketplace or marketplace. Friedman (1999) says that people are affected by the pressures, restrictions, and possibilities that exist within the globalization system, either directly or indirectly. Individuals must interact with these influences while remaining inside the limits of their multinational organization's structure. In order to do business and sustain a connection in the global economy, organizations, and individuals must collaborate on a global scale.

A feature of what the globalization system appears to be generating in the global economy is the phrase Globalization is not Americanization. The political leaders, corporate executives, members of the media, and ordinary citizens have all asserted that globalization is Americanizing the way business is conducted in the international marketplace. According to Joseph (2004) Globalization is not homogenizing and Americanizing the cultures of the world, according to popular wisdom.

The idea of a homogenizing America is based on an erroneously static picture of cultural diversity. The vibrant cultures are continuously evolving and borrowing from other cultures and that borrowing is not necessarily from the U.S. (Taipei Times, 2004). Rather than being static, globalization demonstrates that companies and individuals have the potential to evolve in response to their surroundings, which includes the global economic environment.

The increasingly, multinational businesses are implementing anti-sexual harassment policies that are more in line with established legal standards. This would serve to support the notion that multinational businesses are borrowing from another culture in order to tailor their sexual harassment rules to fit into their own cultural contexts and practices. The corporate access to other nations, as well as the advantages of having a multinational staff, are made possible by globalization. However, difficulties may develop as a result of hiring a diverse workforce, necessitating the establishment of a sexual harassment policy to control the behavior of the employees. Depending on the nation of origin, multiple definitions of sexual harassment may be used (Figure 6.3).

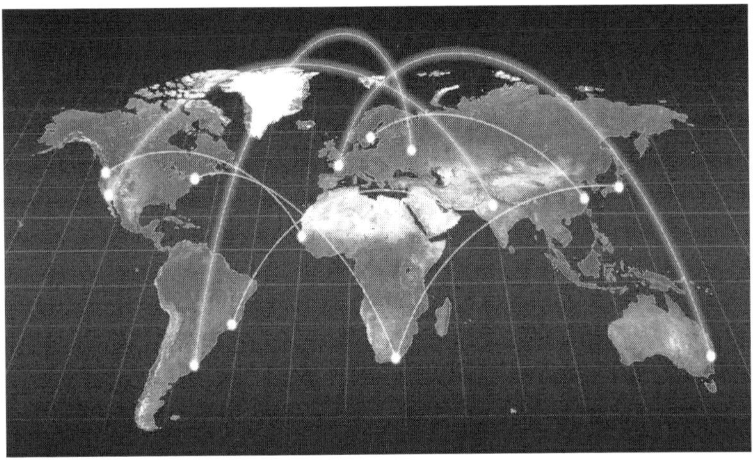

Figure 6.3. Globalization.

Source: Image by Flickr.

6.3.1. Defining Sexual Harassment

Harassment rules contained under corporate codes of conduct cover a wide range of different types of harassment. Sexual harassment is the subject of this study, which will examine one type of harassment that is covered by these policies: sex harassment.

Since it was first used in the 1970s, the term "sexual harassment" has become a household term in American corporate organizations (Kaland and Geist, 1995). Sexual harassment, as defined in the U.S., can take place in two ways: as a kind of exchange of favors or as a hostile work environment.

Quota-based sexual harassment occurs when a condition of employment, such as a pay or promotion, is contingent on an employee agreeing to submit to a sexual advance or engaging in sexual activity with another person.

Failure to comply may result in the termination of the employee's employment (Mulligan and Foy, 2003). It is possible that the most common sort of sexual harassment is the hostile work environment, which is less noticeable than the first type of sexual harassment since it is more prevalent.

Gutek, Cohen, and Konrad (1990) discovered that both men and women engage in social-sexual behavior in the workplace, which are defined as any non-work-related action that has a sexual component. They also discovered that men and women engage in social-sexual activities in the workplace.

These social-sexual actions might be categorized as those that contribute to the concept of a hostile work environment, as described above.

Among the behavior that constitute a hostile work environment include the distribution of sexually explicit pictures, the telling of sexual stories and jokes, the making of obscene recommendations, and any other acts that are regarded improper or unwanted in the workplace (Mulligan and Foy, 2003).

One of the problems with the American concept of sexual harassment is that it places a heavy reliance on the interpretation of judicial precedent. For better or worse, the American definition is dependent on the American court system to determine what is and is not permissible in society.

There are no other ethical criteria offered by international governing organizations that are taken into consideration by the American definition. It is possible that a different term might be more appropriate for understanding the nature of sexual harassment throughout the world.

The Code of Practice of the European Commission provides an alternative definition of sexual harassment, which is broader in scope and defines sexual harassment more vaguely. Physical, verbal, and nonverbal actions are all included in the description of the European Commission Code of Practice, which is made of three main categories of behavior.

The official definition is as follows: Sexual harassment is any unwelcome sexual behavior or other sex-based conduct that has an adverse effect on the dignity of women or men at work. Unwelcome physical, verbal, or nonverbal behavior is included in this definition (Timmerman and Bajema, 1998). Through an examination of the three forms of sexual harassment that occur in society today and the three requirements that constitute the European definition, one will be able to identify the parallels between the American and European definitions.

The verbal harassment is defined by both definitions as the following types of conduct: sexual jokes, comments about one's physical appearance and sexual behavior, requests for sex, and sexual advances made toward a person, whether in written or vocally stated.

Both definitions include physical forms of sexual harassment such as unwanted physical contact, touching of body parts, kisses, and hugs, as well as sexual assault and rape, among other things. According to both definitions, nonverbal forms like gazing, whistling, suggesting gestures, and things such as sexually graphic posters, computer screensavers, and other similar items are considered harassing conduct.

(a) The unwanted, inappropriate, or offensive behavior; (b) refusal or acceptance of behavior impacts decisions regarding a job; and (c) the behavior in issue produces a working environment that is threatening, hostile, or humiliating for the individual were the three factors listed in the definition (Timmerman and Bajema, 1998).

The European concept of sexual harassment provides a more effective means of describing sexual harassment as an issue that is based on ethical norms of behavior than the American one. In other areas of the globe, there are difficulties in defining sexual harassment, making the presentation of a single, global standard problematic.

This is because certain cultures have learnt to tolerate sexual harassment as a normal aspect of conducting business in specific circumstances. Because many cultures do not or have not distinguished certain behaviors as harassing, defining sexual harassment in other parts of the world becomes problematic. This is because many cultures have developed a tolerance for certain behaviors that are considered sexual harassment in other parts of the world.

South Africa, Mexico, and Japan are three countries that have had trouble defining sexual harassment in the workplace. Women in high positions in South Africa did not know whether or not they had been sexually harassed, nor did they know whether or not there were any cases of harassment occurring inside their individual companies (Gordon, 1991). Gordon (1991) reported in it that sexual harassment is viewed differently in South Africa since it is a very subjective notion, and therefore what one individual finds harassing may not be deemed harassing by another individual.

Because of the risk of retaliation from labor regulations, industrial tribunals, and unfair dismissal cases, defining harassment in South Africa becomes a difficult task for companies in the country (Gordon, 1991).

Despite the fact that sexual harassment happens in Mexico, Gordon (1991) asserts that it is normal, or would say accepted, within the Mexican society. Furthermore, according to other studies, sexual harassment happens in Mexican corporate groups, but the act of harassing someone is regarded as a game to be performed. This is a game that many Mexican ladies are accustomed to playing. Quid pro quo harassment has been discovered to be widespread.

Many women do not turn down such offers because they require the work or the money, or because they have no other alternative available to them.

According to Luthar (2002), research done in organizations revealed that sexual harassment was a normal aspect of conducting business in Mexico. Mexican women are accustomed to being approached by a guy about a new promotion or position that is preceded by a sexual favor on their part.

Mexican women are praised by men for their behavior and appearance, according to research conducted by Luthar (2002); and Gordon (1991), who discovered that men are accustomed to performing this social game with the women participating while being aware of the implications and consequences.

According to research data, 95% of women employees in Mexico have experienced sexual harassment at some point in their careers (Mackay, 2001; Carrillo, 1992). Despite the fact that sexual harassment is becoming an issue in Mexico, it is acceptable and allowed due to implicit cultural acceptance for males who believe they are superior to women (Luthar, 2002; Gordon, 1991).

As more and more women enter the profession and demonstrate that they are as capable as males in the job, it is expected that change will occur. In addition, defining sexual harassment in Japan is a tough task. Sexual harassment is a relatively new notion in Japan; therefore, it is difficult to describe.

After the Equal Employment Opportunity Act was passed in April 1986, according to Gordon (1991), attention to sexual harassment began to be paid to it in the Nihon Keizai Shimbun (Japan's equivalent to the Wall Street Journal).

Many organizations in Japan have established contact centers and enlisted the services of ombudsmen to deal with complaints of sexual harassment. Using an American definition, according to information on the Keio University website, it is limiting or improper to describe sexual harassment as such, according to the information.

Sexual harassment is described as more subjective than other types of harassment, making it harder to come up with a specific description. Despite the fact that identifying sexual harassment is difficult, incidents of harassment are still recorded.

Despite the fact that definitions of sexual harassment differ from culture to culture, there are some commonalities that can be used to facilitate the development of an open dialog among organizational members, with the goal of bringing about a change in the way sexual harassment is treated within organizations. Individuals who see a problem and are able to express their concerns to management have the potential to bring about change. Introducing more specific and precise rules will aid in the creation of a more comfortable working atmosphere for all parties involved. It is vital to understand how sexual harassment differs from culture to culture; as a result, it is necessary to define the cultural dilemma that arises when businesses seek to conduct business in a globalized economy.

6.4. GUIDE TO WRITE A CODE OF CONDUCT IN WORKPLACE

6.4.1. A Code of Conduct Sets Company Norms for Behavior

These standards serve as the foundation for a culture of inclusion and diversity. The process of developing codes of conduct should include participation by company executives from all functional areas. This will allow them to think critically about how to establish culture on their teams and how to build bridges with other teams. It also gives a chance to incorporate unique issues, experiences, interactions, needs, and anticipated reactions from diverse groups into the discussion.

Efficacious codes of conduct can only be achieved when they are integrated into a wider process that involves teaching, enforcing them, monitoring, and evaluating them, and continuously evolving them.

6.4.2. The Team Drafting the Code of Conduct Should Believe in Diversity and Inclusion

Idealistically, the team should be diverse and inclusive, and it should include influencers who can help develop corporate support for the code of conduct; alternatively, consider bringing in an outsider to guide the process and assist with communication of the outcomes. Avoid the temptation to copy and paste from the extensive codes of conduct established for conferences and events; these codes of conduct are not intended to address the subtleties and complexity of workplace interactions, and thus should not be used.

6.4.3. The Team Should Carefully Consider the Scope and Enforcement of the Code

Is it only applicable in the office, or does it apply to work-related social gatherings and events as well? Who is covered under this policy? What is the procedure for making a complaint in the event that a violation occurs? What should an employee do if a conflict of interest arises somewhere along the reporting chain?

Codes of behavior are frequently pushed by attorneys, which is a mistake in this case. A lawyer leading the process will almost always result in a risk-mitigation and law-oriented approach, even with participation from a larger multi-disciplinary team. When it comes down to it, what they truly want is a collaborative, values-driven strategy-one that will motivate people to work with openness, trust, and cooperation rather than bias, fear, and avoidance.

6.4.4. The Code of Conduct Is Not a Silver Bullet for Inclusive Workplaces

Codes must be developed and used in conjunction with other supported components in order to be successful. Moreover, if such initiatives fail, we are afraid that businesses would point the finger at one another and reject diversity and inclusion as unimportant.

6.5. SUGGESTIONS TO WRITE A CODE OF CONDUCT IN WORKPLACE

6.5.1. Make the Code of Conduct Comprehensive and Visible

In the first paragraph of the code of conduct, one should include a clear statement of purpose that is based on the mission, values, and operations of their organization. It should be integrated with other rules, such as anti-discrimination and anti-harassment policies, as well as inclusive benefits and confidentiality policies, and it should be consistent across all collaborations with outside organizations, consumers, and suppliers, among other things.

It is essential that codes of behavior be made available to the public, be widely accessible, and be extremely prominent. A code of conduct that is buried deep within a company's internal website is of limited use. In fact, a lack of visibility may be detrimental since it communicates that a firm does not place a high priority on its code of conduct. If the policy is breached, specify the range of possible reactions as well as the procedure for enforcing the policy.

6.5.2. Craft a Statement of Values in the Code of Conduct

It is typically the first thing that people notice when learning about a company's culture that are the values of the organization. A company's values may be a determining factor and lure for skilled workers seeking a matching environment. Existing workers can use the company's values as an abbreviated code of conduct and as a method to check in on whether their actions and experiences are in line with the company's values and mission.

The suggestions for developing strong value statements are:

- Speak in the language of the people they are speaking to. Be a proponent of the concept that the employees will be treated with dignity and empathy as valued members of the working group.
- Provide clear instructions on how and when acts that contravene the code of conduct will be dealt with, as well as on who will be engaged in the enforcement process.
- When at all possible, avoid utilizing internal jargon or language. While doing so, one may guarantee that others outside their organization understand what they are saying, which is beneficial for recruiting fresh talent.
- Preserve core principles by making them obvious, straightforward, and proactive; address more difficult problems such as the anti-harassment policy as separate statements elsewhere in the code of conduct.

6.5.2.1. Specify Who Is Covered

The diversity they wish to see in their firm should be described in a section, with special attention paid to the groups who are frequently targeted for exclusion from the workplace. However, the list should contain the categories of persons who are legally protected from discrimination (known as protected classes), but it should not be confined to these individuals. Discrimination on the basis of race, color, national origin, religion, sex; age; handicap; sexual orientation; gender identity; gender expression; marital status; or medical/genetic condition is prohibited under state and federal law in California, for example.

6.5.2.2. Specify a Process for Reporting Complaints

Develop reporting processes from the standpoint of an employee who has been involved in an event and has to report it, rather than from the perspective of a corporation trying to avoid responsibility. Consider providing more than one way for reporting an event to their customers. It is possible that an incident will be unreported if there is no opportunity to remain anonymous in the event that a circumstance arises in which an employee fears reprisal.

This can result in many instances getting undetected, management being unaware of a repeat offender or a cultural problem, and multiple occurrences remaining unreported. Making conflict resolution simple and non-confrontational can help employees learn to self-regulate and control their own behavior and occurrences.

The inclusion of resources and a commitment to assistance from the firm at the conclusion of this choice helps to mitigate the predicted propensity for a reporter's experience to be diminished. Companies should also make it plain that retribution, whether it comes from within the firm or from those who are the subject of allegations, will not be tolerated.

Employees should be aware of who to report to and how to report, as well as what to do if a conflict of interest prevents them from reporting in the usual manner. Example: If someone's boss is dating her harasser, she may not feel comfortable reporting the incident to authorities. A third-party ombudsperson may be a helpful tool for providing a secure manner to report issues that is separate from the company's internal reporting structure and hierarchy.

Employees should also be informed on what to expect when they file a report, including the many types of consequences that might result from different acts, as well as specific instances of each. In order for them to grasp how the procedure will unfold, they should be given a timeframe.

Managers must follow up with workers at three-month intervals and then again at six-month intervals to assess whether they believe the problem has been handled and to discuss if the inappropriate behavior has been discontinued.

The business's code of conduct and associated rules will be reinforced by these follow-ups, which will ensure that employees are treated with respect and that the organization is comfortable discussing particular concerns and prepared to work on solutions until the problems are resolved. It also emphasizes the importance of the employee's perceptions and experiences in the process, which the firm recognizes may be a long one and may continue for a long time. Managers must be trained on how to receive and handle reports, as well as given direction on how to organize an investigation and resolution timetable. Consider their approach to conflict resolution when they establish a policy on how to deal with complaints and other issues.

6.5.3. Cover What Happens Outside the Workplace

Occasionally, encounters might not reach to the level of overt exclusion or harassment, but they nevertheless express bias, reinforce stereotypes, or draw attention to disparities. The fact that they are awkward makes them equally troublesome since they generate discomfort, make one employee feel uncomfortable at work, and may even cause tension in interpersonal interactions. This should be addressed in their code of conduct, which should be applicable both on and offline.

The environment of work-related social activities such as conferences, happy hours, holiday parties, and industry gatherings can be a source of exclusion and harassment. Career success is frequently dependent on the ability to network and work as a team outside of the organization. It is possible that problem conduct will have a chilling impact on chances for underrepresented groups, as they may be unwilling to engage in off-premises activities, resulting in the loss of potentially important relationships.

6.5.4. Develop a Clear Policy for Offsite Events with Considerations

- ***Location***: When it comes to the venue, is it renowned for being inclusive, or is it known for rejecting service or being insulting to people, particularly those from marginalized communities.
- ***Alcohol***: Will there be alcohol served at the conference or event? Alcohol can inspire individuals to engage in improper behavior. Make non-alcoholic beverages accessible and think about how to deal with (or avoid) those who appear to be inebriated in a straightforward manner. Options might include no hard alcohol, two drinks per employee per day utilizing drink tickets, or an open bar for a set number of hours each day. The policy should be stated and implemented in a clear and concise manner.
- ***Time***: Is the meeting or event scheduled at a time that is appropriate for employees who are responsible for children or dependents, and with adequate notice for them to arrange alternative childcare? When making their plans, keep in mind to include child care and travel support.

- ***Food***: When supplying food, are they taking into consideration religious holidays that may have an impact on their employees' eating habits? Vegetarians, religious or medical limitations, and food labeling are all taken into consideration, so that employees do not have to divulge personal information while choosing their meals.
- ***Invitations***: to social activities, both official and unofficial, should be published in a public and easily available manner, such as through a team's Slack channel and a group email address. The use of ad hoc word-of-mouth planning may exclude people from underrepresented backgrounds and those who do not have strong personal networks inside the firm, according to the authors.

6.5.5. Write and Communicate a Clear Anti-Harassment Policy

It is an inevitable component of every inclusive firm to have an anti-harassment policy in place. It guarantees that, in the case of an occurrence, workers are aware of their rights as well as the procedures that are accessible to them for seeking assistance.

Anti-harassment rules should clearly describe what constitutes inappropriate behavior, specify the procedures to take in the event of an occurrence, and clarify what to expect after a report has been submitted. In order to avoid having several rules for different types of harassment, they should cover all forms of inappropriate behavior in a single document like racial, gender, sexual, etc. Employers who focus on particular types of harassment with their own policies may reduce the impact of other forms of harassment and leave workers in the dark about whether situations constitute harassment.

Employees who have previously worked in less inclusive workplaces may be deterred from repeating specific types of breaches if the repercussions are listed in front of them. Specific concerns covered by the policy might include, for example, the following:

- Confidentiality and trustworthiness;
- Communication methods that are respectful and effective;
- Preferred techniques of operation;
- Professionalism standards must be met;
- The use of company-owned property;
- Use of social media platforms;

- Belittling or subtle indications of prejudice are prohibited;
- Abuse or attack that is verbal, physical, or written;
- Bullying, intimidation, or victimization are all unacceptable;
- Discrimination;
- Harassment;
- Intoxication;
- Misuse of business property or assets in an inappropriate manner;
- Failure to adhere to the company's core principles;
- Engaging in illegal conduct;
- Violations of any other business policies;
- Workplace décor-visual clues may express culture as well as bring cultural baggage with them. Explicit messages about inclusion can be undermined and feelings of exclusion exacerbated by unsuitable or excessively masculine environmental features, for example.

Workplace power dynamics may have a significant impact on how individuals engage with one another and form connections at work, including romantic or sexual ones. Ineffective and unworkable, a policy prohibiting dating can be implemented.

A clear guideline on how and when it is okay to ask coworkers out on dates may be both successful and beneficial for both the company and the employees. Some organizations, for example, have a "one-shot" policy, which means that an employee can only ask another employee out once throughout their employment. If the response is no, the employee is prohibited from asking the question again under this policy.

In addition to a clear policy on relationship disclosure, codes of conduct should provide specific guidelines on how and when relationships should be disclosed. Typically, the senior party (or both, if they are peers) must report the connection to their boss within 24 hours after the first date, according to industry standards.

The firm should consider whether to modify the chain of command or take other measures to alleviate the situation if the parties have a reporting connection with one another. For example, if an engineer begins dating his team boss, it may be necessary to transfer him to a different department.

Some businesses forbid direct reporting ties from developing into romantic or sexual partnerships. They should decide where they want their company's policy to be, and they should make sure that it is understood by all of their workers.

6.5.5.1. Monitor, Audit, and Survey the Results of the Code of Conduct

Monitoring and auditing of the execution of their codes of conduct should be done on a regular basis, with particular emphasis paid to the levels of compliance and efficacy of the enforcement measures in place. Organizations should communicate the findings of these audits to their workers in a manner that protects the privacy of individuals who participated in the audit. The metrics on which companies report include things like suspected breaches, reporting methods, whether or not complaints were substantiated, and the company's response.

The code must also be up to date, which means that it should be inspected at least once every six months to see whether any improvements are necessary. If the legislation, rules, and ethical standards have changed, it may be essential to update the system.

Not all information regarding how effectively a code of conduct is operating can be obtained through audits, for example. Employees should be requested to provide feedback on business surveys, performance evaluations, and when they make complaints so that management may improve the firm (Figure 6.4).

Figure 6.4. Diversity and inclusion in workplace.

Source: Image by Wikimedia.

6.6. EFFECTIVELY COMMUNICATING ANTI-HARASSMENT POLICY

What steps is their company taking to maintain a safe and accountable workplace in the light of numerous accusations of sexual harassment in the media and online.

This is not a brand-new problem. A survey by the society for HR management found that 94% of firms in the U.S. had harassment and/or bullying policies in place that specify behavior that is forbidden.

However, if they believe that having a policy is sufficient, think again. The results of an EEOC research on workplace harassment conducted in 2016 indicated that regulations alone do not promote acceptable behavior. According to the findings of the study, roughly 90% of survey participants who had experienced sexual harassment did not submit a formal complaint.

This is a once-in-a-lifetime opportunity to be very explicit about workplace harassment. Making this a priority in their company is in the best interests of all parties involved. The best performance comes from people who feel secure and welcomed in their workplace, and this helps to boost company performance. As they conduct an internal assessment of this matter, keep these communication best practices in mind.

6.6.1. Review and Update the Existing Harassment Policy

Begin by taking a look at the existing policies. When was the last time it was re-evaluated and made more current? If it has been more than five years, it is considered to be too old. In order to be effective, the policy should at the very least include instances of banned activity, describe the mechanism for reporting problematic conduct, and be signed by the current CEO (Chief Executive Officer). Then make certain that the policy, as well as the reporting mechanism, are easily accessible. The bottom line is to let employees know where they may go for assistance.

6.6.2. Time for Leaders to Speak Out

Every leader is responsible for his or her actions. Allow workers to hear it straight from the C-Suite: harassment will not be tolerated in the workplace. HRs can assist with this attempt, but they cannot take on the entire burden. Executives must take the initiative and pledge that, if complaints are made, they will be examined quickly and that necessary steps will be taken as a result of the findings. Communicate that retribution is banned, as many incidents go unreported due to fear of losing their jobs or facing repercussions.

6.6.3. Training

Even though most businesses give online harassment training, do they require that employees finish the course? Is there a section in new employee orientation that addresses harassment? Training will ensure that employees have a better grasp of the types of actions that constitute harassment. Furthermore, the HRs staff must be prepared and ready to undertake quick, impartial, and complete investigations when the need arises.

6.6.4. Amplify the Message Through Internal Communications

If an employee is subjected to sexual harassment or observes it, do they know what to do and how to report it? Individuals should be able to report with ease. Spread the word about the harassment policy and reporting procedure through a variety of media. It should be discussed at town halls and on blogs, as well as in a video from the CEO, and a link to it should be placed on the front page of their corporate intranet. Declare it clearly to ensure that everyone understands that harassment is not tolerated in their company's culture.

6.6.5. Communicate the Policy and Train Employees

Apart from distributing policies to each employee, it is recommended that the policies be read and discussed to employees at group meetings. Employees should be trained on how to detect and deal with harassment in the workplace. It is essential that managers and supervisors be trained in the enforcement of company policies, are made aware of wrong conduct among employees when it occurs and are taught on the right steps to take to avoid and rectify inappropriate behavior.

6.6.6. Communicate the Policy More Than Once

In order to be an effective weapon against sexual harassment, the policy must be conveyed to workers on a regular basis and in plain language. This may be accomplished professionally through staff meetings and informally through interactions between managers and supervisors and their subordinates.

The communication process can be aided by managers and supervisors requiring employees to attend training, following up with employees on what they learned at training, inviting questions about the training and policy, as well as providing positive responses to employees who participate in the company's efforts to prevent and eliminate sexual harassment in the workplace.

Immediately following the announcement of a policy against sexual harassment, managers, and supervisors must take further steps to ensure that workers are not participating in prohibited behavior. If a meeting is called to order employees to refrain from engaging in a certain conduct, managers, and supervisors should make certain that the meeting was taken seriously by the employees in attendance.

6.6.7. Make Sure the Policy has an Effective Complaint Procedure

When it comes to sexual harassment complaints, a complaint system should encourage employees to come forward with their claims. An employee should be able to raise a first-time complaint to a number of different individuals. It is recommended that HRs personnel or other suitable employer representatives be assigned the task of investigating employee concerns. In the event that one of the prospective investigators turns out to be the suspected harasser, there should be at least two of them. Having both men and women designated as investigators is also a good idea since the complainant may feel more comfortable reporting inappropriate behavior to someone of the same sex.

Managers and supervisors must take any allegation of sexual harassment that they receive seriously and investigate the matter thoroughly before taking any action. In order to comply with EEO regulations, they should submit the complaint to HRs or any other corporate official who is responsible for EEO compliance. They should reassure staff that anybody who submits a complaint will not be subjected to retribution, and that their concerns will be handled as discreetly as possible. They should also assure anybody who lodges a complaint that their claims will be properly examined as soon as possible.

6.6.8. The Employees Knowing a Policy Exists Is Not Enough

To be effective in proactively preventing bullying and harassment and addressing any issues that emerge, they must take efforts to ensure that all leaders and workers are committed to the following principles:

- Recognize the signs and symptoms of bullying and harassment in the workplace.
- and know what to do if they see or experience psychological damage in the workplace.
- Recognize that they are expected to refrain from engaging in bullying and harassing behavior.
- Recognize their own responsibility in stopping others from indulging in these behaviors.
- Be aware of the ramifications of breaking the policy if they do.

6.6.9. Another Key Point to Remember Is That Creating Awareness Is An Ongoing Commitment

A successful communication strategy entails more than just delivering a message once. There should be a variety of options for effective communication strategies. Their inclusion in as many mediums and programs as possible should be encouraged. Of course, they will want to make certain that their rules and their contents are communicated on an ongoing basis.

6.6.10. The Effective Communication Techniques

Ensure that the new and/or revised policies and procedures are communicated in several ways. Remember, the more methods in which workers learn about their responsibilities, the more likely it is that they will remember and be conscious of their obligations.

The following are some examples of effective communication:

- Training in person or through the internet;
- Newsletters distributed by the company;
- Town hall meetings are held every week;
- Meetings to discuss safety issues;
- Emails from the top of the organization;
- Intranet of the company;
- Session around the coffee cup;
- Provide leaders with speaking notes so that they may discuss them during team meetings. When people hear about new policies from their leader, the message has a greater effect and is perceived as more important;

- Communicate the goals and objectives of the organization in terms of psychological health and safety. Instead, then just informing employees on a new or revised policy, it is more effective to inform them of the goals they hope to achieve;
- Revise corporate safety metrics to incorporate psychological safety as well as injuries as a point of comparison. Nothing conveys importance quite like the integration of it into the success of the firm and personal goals;
- Ensure that their HRs department, safety department, and health and safety committees are all informed of their new roles and duties. At the same time, prepare them for the inquiries that they will almost certainly get. As a result, ensure that they are aware of whom to direct employees to for queries and situations that fall outside of their scope of duty.

One will be more successful if they follow these guidelines in putting their new policies and programs into action.

It is important not to let their policy or program roll-out to be a dazzling flash in the pan that fades away too fast. Their ability to maintain a consistent commitment to the use of effective communication strategies will be critical to their success in generating a long-lasting awareness among their staff (Figure 6.5).

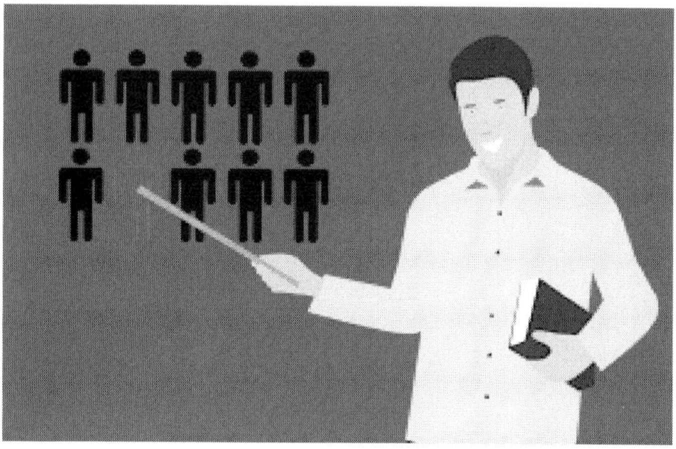

Figure 6.5. Training of employees regarding code of conduct in workplace.

Source: Image by Pxhere.

6.7. CONCLUSION

Cultural sensitivity becomes more important when companies expand their operations across the world and hire employees from a diverse range of cultural backgrounds to support their expansion. Corporations must aim to establish excellent sexual harassment policies; yet only a small number of companies have implemented such policies.

It is important not to let their policy or program roll-out to be a dazzling flash in the pan that fades away too fast. Their ability to maintain a consistent commitment to the use of effective communication strategies will be critical to their success in generating a long-lasting awareness among their staff.

REFERENCES

1. Insight-communication.com. (2018). After #MeToo: Communicating Your Workplace Harassment Policy-Insight Strategic Communications, Inc. [Online] Available at: https://insight-communication.com/2018/02/after-metoo-communicating-your-workplace-harassment-policy/ (accessed on 17 August 2021).
2. Project Include, (n.d.). Guide to Writing a Code of Conduct. [Online] Available at: https://projectinclude.org/writing_cocs#monitor-audit-and-survey-the-results-of-your-code-of-conduct (accessed on 17 August 2021).
3. SHRM, (n.d.). Anti-Harassment Policy and Complaint Procedure (Includes Dating/Consensual Relationship Policy Provision). [Online] Available at: https://www.shrm.org/resourcesandtools/tools-and-samples/policies/pages/cms_000534.aspx (accessed on 17 August 2021).
4. www.employmentlawfirms.com. (n.d.). How to Effectively Implement a Sexual Harassment Policy. [Online] Available at: https://www.employmentlawfirms.com/resources/employment/workplace-safety-and-health/implement-sexual-harassment-policy.htm#1 (accessed on 17 August 2021).
5. Yates, H. T., (2007). Developing and Communicating Better Sexual Harassment Policies Through Ethics and Human Rights. [Online] Scholarworks.umt.edu. Available at: https://scholarworks.umt.edu/cgi/viewcontent.cgi?article=1325&context=etd (accessed on 17 August 2021)

Chapter 7

Sexual Harassment in a Male-Dominated Workplace

CONTENTS

This chapter sheds light on one of the most prevalent and common issue that is the sexual harassment at workplace which is dominated by men. It begins with stating the rules, acts, and policies made for workplace sexual harassment. It then explains the several steps a woman must take in order to tackle with sexual harassment taking place against her.

This chapter also puts emphasis on the blue-collar jobs which is dominated by men where there is a lot of cases for sexual harassment along with this it tells the different reasons due to which sexual harassment is flourishing that is tolerance and not raising voices.

It addresses the cases of sexual harassment which takes place in different sectors and industries that is construction, mining, military, transportation, etc., and states the various factors that contributes to this issue. It also throws light on the different types of sexual harassment at work place, its combating and preventing as well as the anti-harassment policy and trainings.

7.1. INTRODUCTION

Sexual harassment, refers to any form of unwanted sexual behavior that is offensive, humiliating, or frightening. Most significantly, it does not obey the law, instead it defies it. Being sexually harassed influences people in various ways. If someone is experiencing harassment, there are different things that can be done in order to cope with it.

Sexual harassment can be of different types, such as written, verbal, or physical, and can happen physically or even online. Mostly, sexual harassment takes place at workplaces.

When it comes to sexual harassment, both men and women can be the victims. But it happens at workplace more because it is often male-dominant, it might amount to sex discrimination.

Sexual harassment when done to someone, looks like:

- Touching inappropriately, grabbing, or making other physical contact with someone without their permission;
- Someone making comments or texting in a way that implies a sexual meaning;
- Asking somebody for sex or sexual favors;
- Staring at someone in a way that makes the other person uncomfortable;

- Showing somebody rude and offensive material so that they or others can see it;
- Making gestures that are sexual or suggestive body movements towards someone;
- Cracking jokes that are sexual and comments around or directly to an individual;
- Questioning someone about their sex life;
- Insulting someone with comments that are sexual;
- Committing a criminal offence against an individual, such as making a vulgar or filthy phone call, lewdly revealing themselves or assaulting someone sexually.

7.2. SEXUAL HARASSMENT IN THE CONTEXT OF DOUBLE MALE DOMINANCE

It has been said that male-dominated workplaces have been numerically propagating cultural norms and that also support sexual bravado, sexual posturing, and the denigration of feminine behavior. To increase the risk of sexual harassment these cultural norms has been shown and they are also considered as the features of the normative male dominance.

It has been said that on the sexual harassment the effect of numerical male dominance may be mediated by the level of normative male dominance in the work environment. To test this assumption was the main aim of this study.

More and more research attention has been received by the sexual harassment since the mid-1970s. At work it has been seen that from the United States (U.S.) meta-analytic data revealed that one out of every four women has experienced sexual harassment at work.

In addition to it, a research has been conducted on the effects of sexual harassment and it shows that sexual harassment is a workplace danger that is not only detrimental to the target's well-being but also brings about organizational costs, such as lowered productivity and morale, higher absenteeism and turnover, and legal fees (Figure 7.1).

Figure 7.1. Offensive contents.

Source: Image by The Blawq.

With the male dominance the sexual harassment has been associated. Therefore, there is no clarity about the mechanism which underlies the relation between sexual harassment and the male dominance.

As the offensive behavior the sexual harassment has been defined and which has a sexual dimension. By Fitzgerald, Swan, and Magley frequently used psychological definition and by the recipient as offensive an unwanted sex-related behavior at work that is appraised, exceeding her resources or threatening well-being.

It has been seen that in the previous research there are three forms of sexual harassment which are notable, which is gender harassment (nonsexual gender-based experiences, such as sexist comments), unwanted sexual attention (uninvited sex-based comments, gestures, or attempts at physical contact), and sexual coercion (work-related intimidation or rewards used to induce sexual cooperation). It has been noted that gender harassment does not refer to sexual behavior and as such may not be considered as sexual harassment.

It has been noted that different models have been proposed with regard to the causes and an etiology of sexual harassment. Important features have been shared by these models. The core problem which is being considered is the power differences between victims and perpetrators. The root causes of the sexual harassment are being regarded by the male dominance and masculine hegemony, which means sexual harassment is used to accomplish or maintain masculinity and status differences between men and women. It has been said that the objective of sexual harassment is not necessarily the pursuit of sex, but rather intimidation and the satisfaction of power needs.

In the organizations the study of sexual harassment recently addresses the relation between sexual harassment and male dominance from a more complex perspective. It has been said that investigation has been done by them on the place of men in sexual harassment, as perpetrators as well as victims, so this means these studies not only focused on how women experience male dominance.

As a multifaceted concept the study has been proposed by the male dominance and also consist of least two dimensions: numerical and normative male dominance. By the men organizations that are numerically dominated and also have many more male than female employees. From a numerical perspective most, research has explored the male dominance in the past e.g., sex-ratio studies.

Therefore, normative male dominance has gained more attention over the last two decades. To an organizational or occupational culture normative male dominance is being referred and that rewards traditional masculine values, such as support of the heterosexual norm, the devaluation of women, sexual bravado, aggression, emotional self-regulation, risk taking, and technological competence.

By many recent empirical studies, the relation between both numerical and normative male dominance and sexual harassment has been supported.

In several ways normative male dominance can be put into the operation, for instance a sexist behavior. Women were denigrated and are not accepted as equally capable as men in an organization, where sexist behavior was tolerated or part of the job.

It has been found that to sexual harassment the sexist behavior is being related and along with this it has been said that women who perceived sexist attitudes and beliefs among male co-workers were more likely to have experienced sexual harassment. In contrast, it has been seen that there are some respondents who perceived their department as positive towards the equal treatment of men and women who experienced less unwanted sexual behavior.

There is another manifestation of the male dominance that is considered as the sexualized organization. By the frequent sexual talking and joking the sexualized work environments are being defined. In the sexualized company's sexual harassment was more prevalent than in the professional companies.

For example, to engage in the sexual harassment of the women interactions between co-workers are more likely to engage and research in a sample of male university faculty and staff revealed that men who report sexualized workplace relations.

In addition to it, in the male dominated organizations it has been said that harassing behaviors are likely to be tolerated, which in turn contributes to the prevalence of sexual harassment. It has been said that potential harassers may perceive that they are free to harass only if the managers tolerate harassing behaviors.

There is research which is being conducted by Hulin, Fitzgerald, and Drasgow in which the assumption has been confirmed. In any of the meaningful way the perceived risk to the victim of complaining, the likelihood that their complaints will not be taken seriously, and the probability that offenders will not be sanctioned and can also increase the incidence of the sexual harassment.

Moreover, it has been seen that sexual harassment is being experienced by the women at higher levels only in those organization where women have believed that is tolerant level. In the same way, with regard to sexual harassment in organizations where more men saw the manager as indifferent or neutral, more women were actually harassed than in organizations where fewer men perceive the manager as indifferent or neutral with regard to sexual harassment (Figure 7.2).

Figure 7.2. Laws for sexual harassment.

Source: Image by The Blue Diamond Gallery.

It has been found that sexual harassment occurs relatively often numerically in the male-dominated organizations, which means in more gender-balanced workplaces women who work in predominately male workplaces experience more instances of sexual harassment than women. It has been seen that sex ratio has been included in their integrated model of the antecedents and as an aspect of job gender context in the consequences of the sexual harassment.

In several empirical studies there is support for this model which was found, for example in the army. It has also been found that as the ratio of male co-workers increases women are more likely to have experienced sexual harassment in the federal workplace. A link between sex ratio and sexual harassment had been found in meta-analytic studies.

The effect of double male dominance has been studied too. According to Baigent (2005), firefighting is a doubly male-dominated occupation. It is numerically dominated by men as male firefighters outnumber female firefighters by far.

In addition, the cultural norms of firefighting are extremely masculinized. Qualitative research among firefighters in the USA has revealed that for aspiring firefighters conquering a place into the existing male-dominated culture is their first priority. In this process senior firefighters acted as gatekeepers to an informal hierarchy of men. It appeared that to socialize female aspirants these gatekeepers had little means but sexually harassing these women (Baigent, 2005).

It seems that numerically male-dominated workplaces propagate cultural norms that support sexual bravado, sexual posturing, and the denigration of feminine behavior (Sbraga and O'Donohue, 2000). These cultural norms are features of normative male dominance, which have been shown to increase the risk of sexual harassment.

This implies that the effect of numerical male dominance on sexual harassment may be mediated by the level of normative male dominance in the work environment. However, to our knowledge this has not been studied empirically. Building on the model of Fitzgerald, Drasgow et al. (1997), many researchers studied the effect of job gender context and organizational tolerance on sexual harassment (Cantisano, Domınguez, and Depolo, 2008; Willness et al., 2007). However, mechanisms that explain why numerical male dominance is a risk factor have not received sufficient research attention. As such it is not yet clear which mechanism underlies the relation between sexual harassment and numerical male dominance.

7.3. ACT AND RULES FOR WORKPLACE SEXUAL HARASSMENT

There are several rules, regulations, and policies that are made and implemented for the sexual harassment at workplace. Each and every organization must follow such acts and policies regarding this. For instance, The Sexual Harassment of Women at Workplace (Prevention, Prohibition, and Redressal) Act 2013 ("the Act") was incorporates after 16 years of Vishaka with the purpose to give security and protection against the sexual abuse and inappropriate behavior done with women at workplace and for the warding off and decompensation of complaints of sexual harassment and for matter associated there with or subsidiary to that.

The Act identifies sexual harassment as an act or behavior which is unasked (either directly or by suggestion) basically, physical contact and proceeding for a demand or request that is made for sexual favors, carrying out sexually colored remarks and comments, showing someone pornography without their consent, it also involves any other unwanted physical, verbal, or non-verbal behavior of sexual nature.

Figure 7.3. Sexual harassment in blue-collar jobs.

Source: Image by PxHere.

Any act of unwanted and sexual nature shall be regarded as sexual harassment. The Delhi High Court in Shanta Kumar vs CSIR (Council of Scientific and Industrial Research) stated that "without a doubt, physical contact or advances would account for sexual harassment given such physical contact is a fraction of the behavior which is sexually determined. A physical contact which has no hushed tones of a sexual nature and is not provoked by the gender of the respondent may not certainly account to sexual harassment" (Figure 7.3).

The Act also gives the conditions under which an act may account to sexual harassment. These include:

- Implemented or directed promise of privileged treatment in a women's employment;
- Implied or direct threat of destructive treatment in the employment of a woman;
- Unstated or obvious ultimatum about a woman's present or future employment status;
- Interruption in the work or making an intimidating or disrespectful or hostile work environment for a woman;
- The insulting treatment done to a woman likely impacts their health and safety as it is like a mental and physical abuse which deteriorates her health overall.

The significant feature of the Act is that it anticipates the framework of Internal Complaints Committee at each and every office of the company or institution, which has more than 10 employees, to listen to the complaints as well as rectify complaints concerning to sexual harassment.

Where the total number of employees are not more than 10, the Act caters for setting up of Local Committee by the District Officer in each and every district. The committee while examining such complaints might have the same power as lodged in a civil court.

A resentful woman can file a written complaint to ICC that is Internal Complaints Committee, from three months from the date of the incident taking place and in case of sequence of these types of incidents within three months from the last incident which is of this type.

Although, any detainment in filing the complaint can be disregarded by the committee up to the time period of three months further. If there is a case of physical or mental inability of the aggrieved woman, her legal successors or such other person as explained in Rule 6 of The Sexual Harassment of Women at Workplace (Prevention, Prohibition, and Redressal) Rules, 2013 ("the Rules") is capable of making or filing a complaint.

On receiving the complaint, the committee, prior to commencing an inquiry, might take steps to resolve the matter and cases between the aggrieved woman and the respondent by means of appeasement and when a settlement is obtained no further inquiry is supervised. If the conciliation fails or any term of the settlement received at has not been observed with by the respondent, the committee shall move further in addition to the inquiry.

In the series of the cases of a domestic worker, the Local Committee shall, if the case of professional misconduct exists that is prima facie, taking further the complaint to the police, in the time span of seven days for filing the case under Section 509 of Indian Penal Code or any other significant provisions of the said Code wherever relevant.

The cases where both the parties are employees, the postulates of natural justice are followed and both the parties are listened to properly and opportunity is provided to create a portrayal in opposition to the findings of the committee.

For the purpose of carrying out an inquiry, the committee must possess the similar powers that are lodged in a civil court. The committee has to finish the scrutinization within a time span of 90 days. The committee can meanwhile give specific reassurance to the aggrieved woman in the course of the county of the inquiry.

The committee in the time span of 10 days after fulfillment of the inquiry shall cater to the report of its detection to the employer or District Officer and the apprehensive parties. When the claims in opposition to the respondent have been demonstrated the committee must advocate the employer or District Officer to take proper action for the cases dealing with sexual harassment as misconduct in conformity with provisions of service rules and sometimes where such rules are not made or implemented, as authorized in Rule 9 of the Rules and to pay this amount of money to the aggrieved woman as it is regarded appropriate, in conformity with the Section 15 provisions, from the pay of the respondent. The employer or the District Officer shall act upon the proposal within 60 days.

In case of filing a complaint, which is distorted or malicious and the cases based on false evidences the committee might suggest to the employer or District Officer to take action in conformity with the service rules and regulations provision or at places where service rules of such kind do not exist, in such way as formulated in Rule 10 of the Rules.

In opposition to the recommendations made by the committee, an appeal can be filed before the court or tribunal, within the time span of 90 days from the date of recommendations, in compliance either with service rules or without the service rules, to the Appellate Authority of the Industrial Employment (Standing Orders) Act, 1946, under Section 2.

There exists a prohibition when it comes to the publication of identity of the aggrieved woman, witnesses, respondent, and contents of the complaint, examination proceedings and the recommendations of the committee, excluding the information related to the justice provided to any victim of sexual harassment. Upon the violation of Section 16 of the Act, such person must be responsible for penalty in conformity with service rules in addition to the absence of service rules, in conformity with Rule 12.

The Act provides specific duties which is applied on the employer as well as on the District Officer under Sections 19 and 20 sequentially, such as establishing awareness at workplace regarding the context of sexual harassment, stimulating the feelings of the employees, address the complaints committee in carrying out the inquiry, obey with the recommendations that is framed by the committee, monitor time to time submissions of reports that is constructed by the committee, etc.

The disagreement of the provisions of the Act done on the employer's part might result in a penalty which may expand to 50,000 rupees and has the ability of also conducting to cancellation of their license or at times withdrawal, or failure to renew or approve, and even the cancellation of the registration, as per the existing case.

Regardless of the Act is in force during the year 2013, the awareness in context of the outcomes of sexual harassment as well as its amends against the same is restricted. The effectual and efficient implementation and execution of POSH Act not only needs to establish an environment where women can speak up about the wrongdoings done against them, their grievances and humiliation without being scared and get justice but also making men sensitive towards treatment of women and the unjust behavior that women had to face at workplace is fairly obligatory.

7.3.1. What a Women Must Do After Facing Sexual Harassment at Workplace

The term bystander intervention is implemented in order to illustrate the situation when it takes place, that is, if a person comes across a circumstance and expresses their opinion about language and/or behavior of someone else which is inappropriate, disrespectful, abusive, and dangerous. Bystanders are capable of preventing sexual violence when they identify a situation could mount and interfere. For instance, reaching out and helping someone who might be in need for assistance as they can be in danger or at risk for sexual assault. Bystander intervention can also prove to be a beneficial strategy if one encounter or be the viewer of sexual harassment. One does not have to be a hero so as to make a positive influence in anybody's life, and an individual is capable of interfering in a manner that fits their level of comfort and is relevant for the situation.

If an individual decides to step in, they might be able to provide the person who is being harassed a chance to either get them a secure place or walk away from such situations. Mentioned below are a few of the steps one can take if they come across a situation where a person is being sexually harassed while keeping one's own safety in mind at all times, when jumping into such circumstances.

7.3.2. Create a Distraction

One should try their best in order to break into the scene of harassment, or can divert those who are indulged in the harassment. But before doing so, the foremost mandatory thing is to make sure that one should not put themselves in danger in an attempt to save somebody else. In case, someone appears as if they could become violent, then do not be a mode of drawing their attention.

7.3.3. Ask Directly

Another way to prevent harassment is to talk straightaway to the person who is being harassed. Observe their behavior and see if they are acting strange, not willing to go to their workplace, ask them if someone is humiliating them at work, or if they are having any kind of trouble working there, promise them to provide assistance anytime they run into their harasser. There are little gestures through which one can help their friends or colleagues. For instance, if a friend is anxious or afraid walking alone to their car at night, provide help to walk to the parking area along with them.

7.3.4. Refer to an Authority

The most secure way to step in for both the parties, a person saving and the person who is being harassed might be to bring in an authority figure. One can have conversation with anybody who is often willing to step in such as another employee, security guard, bartender, RA in a dorm, or even a bouncer.

7.3.5. Enlist Others

It can often get difficult to step in alone, mostly in cases where a person is concerned about their own safety and security or in cases, where helping the victim alone is not really possible in such cases, it becomes necessary to take the help of a friend, a colleague or some bystander who are willing to provide their assistance in order to save the victim.

7.4. BREAKING INTO THE BLUE-COLLAR BOYS' CLUB: MALE-DOMINATED, LOW-, AND MIDDLE-WAGE SECTORS

In fields that are conventionally dominated by men, sexual harassment is a very common and extensive issue.

However, sexual harassment is a prevalent term across various sectors, especially in organizations and workplaces. Studies have discovered that factors that are organizational instead of individual, are said to cause sexual harassment more, such as workplaces that are male-dominated, job duties that have been seen as traditionally masculine, a management which is mostly unconcerned, and a climate that pays no heed to an offensive behavior, strongly anticipate harassment. Harassment grows because of such tolerance which prevails and when there is nobody to raise their voices, they stay silent even while going through harassment or while witnessing it.

Researchers have evaluated that women worker up to 40 to 80% go through sexual harassment that is done by men in the workplace. The higher cases of sexual harassment emerge in societies which are traditionally dominated by men, and the hierarchical organizations whereby men enjoy being the foremost, and are accountable for higher positions of power.

Out of all the charges of sexual harassment, approximately 12% were filed between the year 2005–2015, with the EEOC. Mostly all these cases took place in the manufacturing sectors that were male-dominated which demonstrates the third highest cases of those sections associated with complaints, as stated in accordance with the analysis done by the Centre of American Progress.

According to the recent surveys conducted by the RAND (Research and Development Corporation) corporation for the Department of Défense, one out of five active-service women had gone through either sexual harassment or have faced gender discrimination in the former years. Generally, a work environment which is sexually hostile, has had up to 7% of active-duty men.

One study discovered that in past one year, 88% of female construction workers has disclosed and filed complaint against sexual harassment. Whereas, another study found out that one-third women and 37% of LGBTQ (lesbian, gay, bisexual, and transgender queer) workers employed in construction trades have reported harassment quite a lot of times. Among the women firefighters, 88% of them have experienced harassment while working, in the course of their careers and according to a survey, at present 69% of them were being harassed.

Talking about other sectors, sexual harassment is most of the times not about sex at all. A study stated that out of 10, nine women were in the framework of male-dominated domains, which includes the military as well as law, for instance, who have experienced harassment in the dimension of gender put-downs, sexist, or offensive comments, had virtually no unnecessary sexual proceeds. That, as stated by researchers, is a crystal-clear demonstration that the harassment in these domains is framed so as to ensure women feel unwanted, unfit, and not capable of doing the job (Figure 7.4).

Figure 7.4. Masculine identity threat.

Source: Image by Noun Project.

7.5. HARASSMENT FLOURISHES BECAUSE OF TOLERANCE AND SILENCE

According to a report of Pew Research Centre in 2017 discovered that 62% of women who worked in workplaces that were male-dominated, in the workplace, an abundance of women, stated that sexual harassment was the greatest hurdle in their place of work. Almost half of them said harassment in the working environment was the main issue, whereas 28% said they have experienced and faced it personally.

The comparatively less heed was given to sexual harassment taking place in blue-collar settings or in other words in the corporate or industrial sector in the wake of #MeToo media coverage that became popular and was a platform where one can raise their voices. It was a kind of movement that was made in an attempt to throw light on the prevalent conditions that had a work environment which was traditionally driven by men.

7.6. LOW-WAGE AND MIDDLE-WAGE, MALE-DOMINATED BLUE-COLLAR JOBS

7.6.1. Construction and Mining

Construction and mining organization include carpenters, laborers, electricians, pipelayers, equipment operators, roofers as well as highway maintenance workers.

7.6.2. Manufacturing

Manufacturing industry includes fabricators and assemblers, welders, machinists, operators in printing press, operators in sewing machine, inspectors, and sorters.

7.6.3. Law Enforcement

Correctional officers, the patrol officers of police and sheriff, detectives as well as criminal investigators, firefighters, and security guards comprise the law enforcement sector.

7.6.4. The Military

Military consists of active duty, reserve enlisted in the Army, Marine Corps, Air Force and Navy.

7.6.5. Transportation

The transportation sector consists of taxi drivers and chauffeurs, as well as bus drivers.

7.6.6. Other Sectors

Other sectors comprise of Janitors and building cleaners in addition to the agriculture section which includes food processing workers.

7.7. FACTORS CONTRIBUTING TO SEXUAL HARASSMENT

Enclosed in the framework of low as well as middle-wage, the jobs and services that are male-dominated, there prevails numerous themes that amalgamate with multiple types of job in addition to this it anticipates or contributes to the probability of sexual harassment in these frameworks.

7.7.1. Masculine-Identity Threat

According to the research done by Lilia Cortina, who is a professor of psychology at the University of Michigan, along with her colleagues, contends in a male-dominating framework the harassment of women in is an attempt to disrespect and throw women out of workplaces is the factor because conventionally the workplace is seen as a place which belongs to only men and the opinions or work of women are less appreciated instead of a sexual forerunner, as was initially theorized. On the other hand, Legal scholar named Katherine Franke states that in these types of environments sexual harassment can be an instrument both to police as well as disciplines the gender outlaw, the woman who goes out of her way and does the work or job of a man or tries to act superior to men are costed too much, in other words, they have to pay for their doings or actions.

The deck is stacked beforehand against women in conventional male professions. Research has discovered that women are more certainly not liked much in such type of framework or settings, along with this, their faults are more brutally judged as compared to the male colleagues which leads to the questions of competency and elevated job susceptibility. The largest employer in the country, that is the U.S. military, consists of one of the increased rates of sexual harassment cases which is more than any other profession. In an effort to comprehend the reason why the issue of gender and sexual harassment is so widespread at every workplace, researchers have demonstrated numerous prospective factors. In which, one of which is the traditional macho, meaning to say, the "warrior culture" which proves to be bitter and unkind to women viewing them as invaders and outsiders (Figure 7.5).

Figure 7.5. Sexual harassment at work.

Source: Image by Pxfuel.

Women constitute merely 16% of the active services recruiting forces, and among officer corps up to 18%. Various other factors that might incorporate a statistics and records of men who are mainly young, and single and are a part of a lower-ranking positions, a challenging and comprehensive way of living of combats implementations, flexibility, drinking to a great extent, a climate that is organizational, which indulges in sexual as well as in other dispositions of active-duty enlisted forces and 18% of the officer corps.

Other factors may include a demographic of largely young, single men in lower-ranking positions, a demanding and intensive lifestyle of combat deployments, mobility, heavy drinking, an organizational climate that tolerates sexual and other forms of hostility (in the form of aggression, in a combat framework, is prime factor in order to carrying out the job successfully), in addition to this, a hierarchical structure that makes reporting very hard.

7.8. SEXUAL HARASSMENT PERPETRATORS

The lawyers, Kim, and Fiske during 1999 backed up the perspective that, whatever shape it takes, sexual harassment is mostly about the dominance of male and superiority. A majority of former writers typically support that notion. In the year 1979, MacKinnon implied that the unequal status given to women in the workplace can at times lead to sexual harassment.

It was described by Benson during the year 1984 and Grauerholz in the year 1989 that even men in inferior roles of social and economic aspects sense that they have the chance of harassing women, which eventually implies an instance of male sense of dominance.

Tangri, Burt, and Johnson in the year 1982 illustrated sexual harassment as a mode of performing an unequal interconnection of male-female which fundamental to the constructed sex status behavior. This is constructed in the workplace in order to maintain dominance there and can sometimes lead to economic discrimination as well as emotional damage.

This conduct might also result in the different behaviors of women as they become proclaimed, demotivated, or lead to their withdrawal from work. According to the reports of Burgess and Borgida in 1997, women face unnecessary sexual attention such as harassing, receiving threats, unpleasant behavior, and disrespectful conduct more as compared to men.

In 2000, Matchen, and DeSouza examined a unique perspective of sexual harassment in the domain of university. It is generally assumed most likely the sexual harassment perpetrators were male professors. On the other side of the coin, these scholars stated that sometimes female professors might also be victims of sexual harassment which is done in the hands of male students.

They found out that male professors acquired casual unwelcomed attention which is mostly sexual, but seem to experience sexual harassment in real sense from students which is approximately about the same rate as faced by females.

The authors contend that the various dimensions of studies taking place in future should look upon men who are the victims of harassment done by women or in some cases by other men and also it should tell why they do not speak up against it or report it (as suggested by Waldo, Berdahl, and Fitzgerald, in 1998).

The authors also stated that there might be a requirement to establish policies that are direct and obvious and also demoralize sexual activity by either faculty or students. There is a requirement on the part of faculty members in order to know that they can take relevant action in case they are being sexually harassed by their students in spite of the gender or sex of the perpetrator.

7.9. HARASSMENT OF WOMEN IN MALE-DOMINATED SETTINGS

A study, which is done in context of the women in male dominated and masculine cultures, discovered, and stated that men make use of the oppression of women, as a method to associate to other men, and flaunt their masculinity at the same time fortifying the inferior status of women and they also make fun of women, their body, they downplay women, and play along their conduct about sexual harassment so as to fit in the frame and be the superior guy and they do this so that they can acquire the higher position in the male group which is obtained only by demeaning and harassing women.

7.9.1. Isolation and Exclusion

The work environment which is male-dominated are distinguished by either "hyper-masculine" or the cultures of locker room, that proves to be competitive and hostile and are concealed from the scrutinizing eyes of the public or superiors.

The work environment where women are treated as an outsider and are said to contribute only a small part in the workforce, are most of the times, distant, and abandoned such as the military foundations or ships and a few of the production, construction, and agricultural sectors which can be responsible for enabling harassment to take its base and flourish.

In the, trucking industry which is conventionally masculine, whereby the fraction of women is only up to 6% of the workforce, to acquire a commercial driver's license, few of the trucking organizations need trainees to spend at least 28 days with a driver who is more experienced alone when it comes to driving on the road.

In such an example, Karen Shank, who is a trainee driver, was awarded with $1.5 million in destructions after she prosecuted CRST (customer requirement support team) trucking for going through continuous sexual harassment as well as assault on the road together with her trainer.

Few of the women in these environments are also many times not made the part of or are not included when it comes to networks of information that identify who seeks the details about jobs, who is put into account for the most desirable shifts, in addition to who gets promoted.

An inspection by Frontline recorded how workers employed in agricultural, food plant, and janitorial sectors often work in isolated and distant conditions, mainly at night, on extensive, dispersed farms, looking after or preparing plants, or sometimes empty buildings. A study that occurred in California in 2010 on "farm working women" discovered that 80% of women had gone through some sort of sexual harassment, and examinations in the agriculture industry done by Bernice Yeung and Frontline's 'Rape in the Fields' and 'Reveal News' states indigenous mass rape, sexual assault, as well as harassment with few of the prosecutions.

7.9.2. Normalized Harassment Cultures

Talking about the areas of police and sheriff's patrol officers, women constitute only up to 14%. According to a study, "Survival in all Boys Club" discovered that sexual harassment is a common and constant thing in such sectors. Despite this fact, only a few cases of harassment are reported by the officers of the female law enforcement.

The main reason for this is, the issue of harassment has become so common and usual that many women do not even consider this as something unusual or negative. Secondly, they are more worried about fitting in the workplace and proving to their male colleagues that they are capable of doing the job no matter what. When a sexually harassed victim makes a complaint which is formal, in consequence to the complaint, vengeance is common and extremely critical.

Likewise, the Centre for American Progress' discovered various other conventional male-dominated work, as most of the manufacturing jobs, for instance as machinists as well as craft workers have been male-dominated from a prolonged period of time, women who enter in such sectors might not have any kind of power or be viewed as outsiders, therefore, this makes women and easy target for harassment.

According to research, black women in blue collar jobs have always been a topic of discussion, as they are possibly exposed to dreadful harassment as compared to the other blue-collar workplaces that are dominated by men. The foremost reason is that they are perceived as not only an outsider but also sexual and racial invaders.

For instance, Judith Vollmar, who was a machine operator, and one of a handful of women who operated in Pennsylvania, in a manufacturing performance fastener at a plant. According to the records of the court, she filed a complaint of a workplace which dealt with sexually blunt images, demeaning signs, co-workers ogling at her every time, making vulgar remarks as well as comments that were sexist, using abusive words for her quite a lot of times at a workplace.

Most of the time, she was told she did not know how to do the job, or how to handle it in the context of carrying out the work. She complained to her supervisor but was suspended on a different basis. In a view of dismissing her case, the firm debated that such type of conduct was typical when it comes to the blue-collar environments.

To which a federal district court judge contradicted, stating, "That a specific workplace is regarded 'blue collar' whatever that is expected to imply, does not vindicate an employer of promoting a workplace which is aggressive and bitter to the female employees."

7.10. ROLE OF BLUE COLLAR TEMP WORKERS IN MALE-DOMINATED WORKSPACE

In highly functioning male-dominated jobs or services, women might also be more apparently excluded from the apprenticeship plans and strategies due to an environment which is hostile, and therefore refused to be given accessibility to one prime medium of economic improvement in the framework of these sectors.

In construction sector, that is one of the most male-dominated when it comes to the private-sector industries, where the ratio of women is less than 3% of construction workers and hardly 2% of the contributor in federally-administered apprenticeships that is the construction apprenticeship programs are most of the time proves to be a significant instrument panel in the domain of a construction career.

Even then, women rarely are able to finish off their apprenticeship programs. One of the reasons for their walking off from these programs are the aggressive work environments, frequent harassment, the absence of child care facilities. This was stated by the National Women's Law Centre, which labeled the construction sector as "the industry that time forgot."

7.10.1. Taxing Physical Demands and Danger

Harassment, heckling, and bullying as well as the ensuing revenge against anybody who stood up and spoke about sexual harassment. Raising voices against these issues must be menacing and specifically in work environments that are abandoned and are physically terrifying. Some of the practices and policies in the sectors that are male-dominated are framed in order to keep women safe and secure by allowing them to speak up against the brutalities done to them.

For instance, meticulous, and arguable entrance exams of physical agility that put their focus upon the upper body force are a fraction of what holds up the numbers of women in the roles of law enforcement, proves to be low. Few of the departments needs recruits to scale walls that are of six-foot, weight lifts the counterpart of their body weight, or need motorcycle attendants in order to physically lift up a motorcycle that is overturned.

An Osha review held in the year 1999 of construction workplaces discovered that sexual harassment, aggressive working conditions, and other aspects such as the unavailability of sanitary toilets, tools, secure clothing in proper sizes of women, and insufficient training were all important workplace pitfalls that restricted the capacity of women to carry out their jobs harmlessly and carefully.

As stated by the female construction workers in the New York Times that they have had instruments relinquished upon them, electrical power surprisingly turned on, while according to the report of one woman where she told that being abandoned atop a 200-foot wind turbine through her male colleagues.

A woman confessed in the Massachusetts Coalition for Occupational Safety and Health, that while working in a manufacturing plant, on denying the advances of the manager, the terrifying condition she faced was that she was made to operate a dangerous machine in which she was not even trained, and in doing so, her hands were burned.

7.10.2. Legal Status

In the industries of agriculture, forestry, poultry, hunting, and animal production, women constitute 23% of the workforce. These industries are responsible for around 1% of EEOC sexual harassment assertations.

There is, however, great reason to reckon specifically gross declaration of harassment because of the pervasiveness of undocumented workers, who are legally as well as economically at risk, in addition to this physically abandoned on rural, and large farms, or plants implemented in food processing where they might have to work all along the night.

Out of the evaluated, in the US, 2 million agricultural workers, an approximated half up to 70% does not possess papers of legal immigration.

Although the workers at times live in labor camps that is given by the employer, who might also cater to their needs of transportation, workers, mainly the undocumented workers, relying on their employer and are more exposed to abuse as well as retaliation. Also, due to the fact that at times individuals coming from the same family work with the same employer, therefore, the complaints about sexual assault and harassment can have unpleasant outcomcs such as it might rcsult in family unemployment, destituteness, more rapes, and assaults in the family, expelling, or various other methods of retaliation.

7.11. SEXUAL HARASSMENT AT WORK

In the past years, the omnipresent and the consequence of sexual harassment, an abstract of discrimination based upon sex, has become an evolving concern at the national as well as the international level. The ILO illustrates sexual harassment as a sex-based conduct that is unasked, disrespectful, and offensive to its recipient.

For sexual harassment to subsist these two circumstances must be prevalent. Sexual harassment might take two shapes: (1) Quid Pro Quo, that is when a job benefit, for instance a rise in salary, or a promotion, or even constant employment is at times made contingent on the victim accepting to demands in order to engage in some sort of sexual conduct; or; (2) disrespectful working environment in which the behavior establishes conditions that are intimidating or disgrace for the victim. A conduct that proficient as sexual harassment.

7.11.1. Physical

Physical violence, such as touching inappropriately, unwanted close proximity which is not even required, etc.

7.11.2. Verbal

Comments, remarks as well as constant questions about appearance, the shape of the body, life-style, sexual inclination, offensive, and disrespectful phone calls.

7.11.3. Non-Verbal

Non-verbal harassment includes whistling, gestures that are sexually-suggestive, demonstration of sexual materials.

7.12. STUDIES AND SURVEYS

A survey that was carried out in Hong Kong in February during the year 2007 portrayed that almost 25% of workers who were interviewed have gone through sexual harassment in which one-third of them were men. Amidst male workers, merely 6.6% had delineated their grievance (in comparison to 20% of women) due to the reason that they felt too humiliated to face mockery.

As stated by a report in the year 2004 examined in Italy, 55.4% of women in the 14–59 age group documented having been the sufferer of sexual harassment. One out three female workers are put through sexual intimidations for career build-up with 65% of them blackmailed every week by the same harasser, generally a co-worker, manager, or supervisor. In addition to this, 55.6% of women who were being subjected to sexual intimidation had walked out from their job.

Around 40%–50% of women, in the European Union (EU), have stated some kind of sexual harassment at the workplace.

In accordance to a survey that was performed by the Australian Equal Opportunity Commission in the year 2004, 18% of interviewees that were aged between 18 and 64 years stated that they had gone through or encountered sexual harassment in the workplace. Out of those who experienced sexual harassment, 62% of them were physically harassed whereas less than 37% were most likely to speak up and report the abuse or assault.

Research have depicted that the category of women who were mostly at the risk to sexual harassment are young, financially independent, either single, or divorced and have a migrant status. While, for men, those who were most harassed are young, gay, and were either the members of ethnic or racial minorities. A recent and evolving trend is the sexual harassment between people of the identical sex.

7.13. COMBATING AND PREVENTING SEXUAL HARASSMENT

In most of the countries, reports have depicted that effective and efficient action in the workplace against sexual harassment needs an amalgamation of legal structure in addition to this, immense enforcement, sufficiently funded institutions, and a greater awareness of the problems. A substantial number of national governments have adapted significant legislative provisions that address the issue of sexual harassment in the workplace.

7.13.1. Anti-Harassment Policy and Training

Employers should institute programs based on anti-harassment that share their part to a welcoming culture where everybody feels they are worthy team members and also captivate talented and skilled job applicants. An organizational harassment policy must:

- explain harassment and give various instances;
- explain that harassment is not acceptable;
- Describe the harassment reporting system together with a designated HR person for reporting assertions;
- Interact the disciplinary outcomes of harassment;
- Highlight the investigation as well as the remediation process;
- illustrate that the act of retaliation done against employees reporting harassment is not allowed.

Employers grasp employees, and themselves, to greater standards. Everyone is capable of a workplace which is free from damaging harassment, and all employees must be anticipated to behave like professional adults while working on the job domains. Not only can workplace harassment lead to way too high lawsuits, but also it establishes a harmful culture that destroys team unity and disrupts productivity.

7.14. MOST REPORTING SYSTEMS DON'T WORK

The problems lie in every sector in the way companies stimulate to the complaints of sexual harassment. In many frameworks, the system is sometimes built up to fail, with victims needed to report assertations of sexual harassment by means of a strict and typical network of command that sometimes incorporates perpetrators along with their allies.

This effectively and efficiently makes the victim silent, suppresses their voices or freezes complaints. This has been a specific major hurdle in the military, though attempts have been made to enable the confidential reports which are to be made out of the chain of command.

But that only makes certain a stopgap measure or estimate which is of enabling the victim to obtain a back-up or in other words support, though not that the perpetrator will be counseled or given severe punishments or the culture that supports harassment will be transformed.

In the technological domain or sector, few of the male-dominated start-ups go along so randomly that human resources (HRs) as well as the policies related to the sexual harassment are an afterthought, at its best. In low-wage frameworks in particular, the scheme and policies along with the reporting systems are most of the times murky. And most of the workers, due to the type of job they have (that is the agricultural work) or legal status (that is undocumented), contain no accessibility to the reporting at all.

7.14.1. Requirement of More Data

In outlining this document, the struggle to find robust, constant data, on the different levels that is national, industry, along with the organizational level that regularly and logically documented the extreme level of sexual harassment especially in the American workplace.

Struggles have been made in order to find solid research on the effectiveness of the weaponry reactions to it. Proceeding further, one need more high-quality data and analysis on all other levels, to additionally throw some light on sexual harassment and to increase a variety of functional solutions that operate across various other sectors and workplaces.

7.14.2. Solutions Must Be Targeted and Aimed at Changing Culture, Systems, and Structures

According to a study, companies or workplaces generally have three primary reactions to combat sexual harassment and they are avoiding complaints and harassment, firing a harasser, and offering training so as to deal with sexual harassment. These approaches and dimensions do not work and does not prove to be effective.

Firing a harasser might solve a particular problem in the short duration of time. Providing a canned, digital sexual harassment training, as is the conduct, might provide security to an organization from legal liability, but does a very little to transform its culture, as nothing changes in the workplace. Ignoring complaints and failing to identify sexual harassment establishes toxic cultures that does nothing good but normalizes sexual harassment.

7.14.3. Women Are the Most Common, But Not the Only, Targets for Sexual Harassment

There are fundamental structures for sexual harassment, but those frameworks do not captivate the differences in experience by various other groups of people as well as by workers in various other sectors. The data demonstrates that among all sectors, women who have a lower status are the most usual targets of sexual harassment in the hands perpetrators, who are generally men having higher status in the society and at workplace as well.

But mostly sexual harassment taking place in the workplace is by no medium restricted to this factor and dynamic. Men, specifically those who do not follow the conventional masculine beliefs, and others ae viewed as outsiders or invaders, such as LGBTQ and gender non-conforming people, can be the easy and common targets.

Women can be harassers as well. People of color, mainly women of color, are more likely to be a victim to sexual harassment as compared to their white counterparts (as stated earlier).

7.14.4. It Is Not Just Bosses and Co-Workers Who Are Doing the Harassing

In almost each and every sector, studies have found out that it is not just managers, or supervisors, or those holding power and higher status are the ones who sexually harass targets. Harassment can also come from coworkers or colleagues, as is the case for some aggressive and disrespectful work environment assertions.

Sexual harassment is also usually done from third parties which is also an issue, as in the context of fast-food restaurant workers, working in the low-wage domain, who can be harassed by customers, and for nurses, doctors, in addition to the healthcare workers who can be harassed even by patients. It is also true for lawyers who are highly paid, who can also be sexually harassed in the hands of opposing counsel, clients, and even judges, in most of the cases.

7.14.5. Sexual Harassment Is Systemic

Sexual harassment is not something that just takes place because of fleeting conditions or desire. It is evident in all sectors through imbalances in power and positions. Men hold significantly more positions of power in all aspects of the economy. Even though in female-dominated areas, men are more likely to be supervisors, managers, and principles. In all fields, racism, and race supplement the next level layer to the imbalances of systemic power.

7.15. CONCLUSION

This chapter gives an insight to the different aspects of sexual harassment that occurs in a male-dominated workplace. It begins with describing the rules, acts, and policies implemented for workplace sexual harassment in addition to this it gives a brief account of what a woman should do after facing it and reducing it by creating distractions, asking directly, referring to authority and enlisting others.

In the second half, this chapter sheds light on the blue-collar jobs which is the most male dominated sector and the rising cases of sexual harassment there, as well as states the different reasons why harassment expands that is due to the tolerance and staying silence while experiencing it constantly.

It talks about the different sectors and industries such as construction and mining, manufacturing, law enforcement, military, transportation, and other sectors like agriculture and transportation where the proportion of men are way to higher in comparison to women also, the cases of sexual harassment go on flourishing in such sectors.

As the chapter proceeds, it states the various factors contributing to this issue, mainly the masculine identity threat and the sexual harassment perpetrators. It describes the cultures that normalized harassment especially in the male-dominated framework together with the taxing physical demands and danger and the legal status.

It discusses the different types of sexual harassment at work which can be physical, verbal, and non-verbal and illustrates the studies and surveys, the combating and preventing of sexual harassment along with the anti-harassment policy and training.

Towards the end of the chapter, it addresses the issues of reporting systems and how they do not work, the requirements of more data, people accountable for causing harassment and the systematic framework of sexual harassment.

REFERENCES

1. 360 Training, (2021). Effects of Sexual Harassment in the Workplace | 360training. [Online] 360 training. Available at: https://www.360training.com/blog/effects-of-workplace-sexual-harassment (accessed on 17 August 2021).
2. Brennan, M., & Rajan, N., (2019). HR issues: Sexual harassment, workplace diversity, cultural sensitivity, privileging, credentialing, denying privileges, difficult conversations. Manual of Practice Management for Ambulatory Surgery Centers, [Online] pp. 239–252. Available at: https://link.springer.com/chapter/10.1007%2F978-3-030-19171-9_16 (accessed on 17 August 2021).
3. De Haas, S., & Timmerman, G., (2010). Sexual harassment in the context of double male dominance. European Journal of Work and Organizational Psychology, [Online] 19(6), 717–734. Available at: https://www.researchgate.net/publication/233093361_Sexual_harassment_in_the_context_of_double_male_dominance; https://www.tandfonline.com/doi/abs/10.1080/09541440903160492 (accessed on 17 August 2021).
4. Glicken, M., & Robinson, B., (2013). Sexual harassment in the workplace. Treating Worker Dissatisfaction During Economic Change, [Online] pp. 59–79. Available at: https://www.sciencedirect.com/science/article/pii/B978012397006000004X (accessed on 17 August 2021).
5. Gössling, S., (2017). Automobility, gender, and sex. The Psychology of the Car, [Online] pp. 103–120. Available at: https://www.sciencedirect.com/science/article/pii/B9780128110089000053 (accessed on 17 August 2021).
6. Gutek, B., (2001). Sexual harassment: Social and psychological issues. International Encyclopedia of the Social and Behavioral Sciences, [Online] pp. 13987–13991. Available at: https://www.sciencedirect.com/science/article/pii/B0080430767039930 (accessed on 17 August 2021).
7. Hatch-Maillette, M., & Scalora, M., (2002). Gender, sexual harassment, workplace violence, and risk assessment. Aggression and Violent Behavior, [Online] 7(3), pp. 271–291. Available at: https://www.sciencedirect.com/science/article/abs/pii/S135917890100043X?via%3Dihub (accessed on 17 August 2021).

8. McLaughlin, H., Uggen, C., & Blackstone, A., (2012). Sexual harassment, workplace authority, and the paradox of power. American Sociological Review, [Online] 77(4), 625–647. Available at: https://www.researchgate.net/publication/234162170_Sexual_Harassment_Workplace_Authority_and_the_Paradox_of_Power (accessed on 17 August 2021).
9. Durana A., Lenhart A., Miller R., Weingarten E., Schulte B. (2018). Sexual Harassment: A Severe and Pervasive Problem. [Online] New America. Available at: https://www.newamerica.org/better-life-lab/reports/sexual-harassment-severe-and-pervasive-problem/breaking-into-the-blue-collar-boys-club-male-dominated-low-and-middle-wage-sectors/#:~:text=A%202017%20report%20by%20the,they'd%20personally%20experienced%20it.; https://www.newamerica.org/better-life-lab/reports/sexual-harassment-severe-and-pervasive-problem/summary-of-findings/ (accessed on 17 August 2021).
10. Rainn, (2021). Sexual Harassment | RAINN. [Online] Rainn.org. Available at: https://www.rainn.org/articles/sexual-harassment (accessed on 17 August 2021).
11. ReachOut Australia, (2021). What is Sexual Harassment? [Online] Au.reachout.com. Available at: https://au.reachout.com/articles/what-is-sexual-harassment (accessed on 17 August 2021).
12. Rifkind, L., & Harper, L., (1994). Conflict management strategies for the equal opportunity difficult person in the sexually harassing workplace. Public Personnel Management, [Online] 23(3), pp. 487–500. Available at: https://journals.sagepub.com/doi/10.1177/009102609402300312 (accessed on 17 August 2021).
13. Sexual Harassment at Work. (n.d.). [eBook] International Labor Office. Available at: https://www.ilo.org/wcmsp5/groups/public/---ed_norm/---declaration/documents/publication/wcms_decl_fs_96_en.pdf (accessed on 17 August 2021).
14. Shah, U., (2019). Sexual Harassment of Women at Workplace: A Brief Analysis of the POSH Act, 2013-Employment and HR-India. [Online] Mondaq.com. Available at: https://www.mondaq.com/india/employee-rights-labor-relations/876830/sexual-harassment-of-women-at-workplace-a-brief-analysis-of-the-posh-act-2013 (accessed on 17 August 2021).

15. Simonit, F., Bassan, F., Scorretti, C., & Desinan, L., (2018). Complex suicides: A review of the literature with considerations on a single case of abdominal self-stabbing and plastic bag suffocation. Forensic Science International, [Online] 290, pp. 297–302. Available at: https://www.sciencedirect.com/science/article/abs/pii/S0379073818304389 (accessed on 17 August 2021).
16. Williams, L., (2013). Adolescence and commercial sexual exploitation. Handbook of Child and Adolescent Sexuality, [Online] pp. 449–468. Available at: https://www.sciencedirect.com/science/article/pii/B9780123877598 (accessed on 17 August 2021).
17. Zhu, H., Lyu, Y., & Ye, Y., (2019). Workplace sexual harassment, workplace deviance, and family undermining. International Journal of Contemporary Hospitality Management, [Online] 31(2), pp. 594–614. Available at: https://www.emerald.com/insight/content/doi/10.1108/IJCHM-11-2017-0776/full/html (accessed on 17 August 2021).

INDEX

D

E